ACADEMIC AND WORKPLACE
SEXUAL HARASSMENT

SUNY Series, The Psychology of Women
Michele A. Paludi, Editor

ACADEMIC AND WORKPLACE SEXUAL HARASSMENT

A RESOURCE MANUAL

O

MICHELE A. PALUDI
AND
RICHARD B. BARICKMAN

STATE UNIVERSITY OF NEW YORK PRESS

Published by
State University of New York Press, Albany

For information, address State University of New York
Press, State University Plaza, Albany, N.Y., 12246

Production by Diane Ganeles
Marketing by Theresa A. Swierzowski

Library of Congress Cataloging-in-Publication Data

Paludi, Michele Antoinette
    Academic and workplace sexual harassment : a resource manual /
Michele A. Paludi and Richard B. Barickman.
        p.   cm.—(SUNY series, the psychology of women)
    Includes bibliographical references and index.
    ISBN 0-7914-0829-9 (CH : alk. paper).—ISBN 0-7914-0830-2 (pbk.
: alk. paper)
        1. Sexual harassment in universities and colleges—United States.
2. Sex discrimination in employment—United States.   3. Sexual
harassment of women—United States.   I. Paludi, Michele Antoinette.
II. Title.   III. Series: SUNY series in the psychology of women.
LC212.862.P35   1991
331.4'133—dc20   90-24364
                                                                      CIP

10 9 8 7 6 5 4 3 2 1

FOR THE SURVIVORS OF SEXUAL HARASSMENT;
WITH HOPE THAT YOUR VOICES CONTINUE TO BE HEARD

Contents

List of Tables

Foreword

In 1982 the Board of Trustees of the City University of New York adopted a policy explicitly forbidding the "harassment of employees and students on the basis of sex." By that time Hunter College, CUNY had already responded to the serious problem of sexual harassment by establishing a special panel composed of faculty, staff, and students to educate the Hunter community about sexual harassment and to investigate complaints. Hunter's Panel on Sexual Harassment continues to serve as a unique volunteer organization composed of people who represent the diversity of our college community. Through their continuing research on the impact and extent of sexual harassment, their educational programs, and their investigation of formal and informal complaints, members of the Panel are the major force in fulfilling our responsibility to create a college atmosphere free of the abusive impact of sexual harassment.

Recently, the members of the Panel have gained national attention through the presentations they have delivered before national and international conferences and through their work as consultants for other campuses undertaking educational programs on sexual harassment or seeking to establish advisory or investigative panels. The authors of this resource manual have worked together as coordinators of Hunter's Panel. Professor Michele Paludi is a distinguished research psychologist who has published a number of works on sexual harassment, developmental psychology of women, and mentoring relationships as they effect women's career development. She directs the research collective on sexual harassment at Hunter. Professor Richard Barickman was one of the original group of faculty and staff who met in order to establish Hunter's Panel and has served as co-ordinator since 1985. He has written on sexual harassment and gender issues in literature. Together they have directed workshops at national conferences—such as the Association for Affirmative Action—and have worked extensively as consultants on academic sexual harassment. During the past few years, their efforts have brought the serious problem of sexual harassment to the attention of college communities throughout the country and they have also suggested ways to improve the college environment and to provide support and redress for those who have been victimized. The resource manual they have written draws upon their experience as researchers, workshop leaders, and consultants, consequently bringing their expertise to an even wider audience.

As the information provided in this resource manual indicates, most female students and some male students as well, can expect to experience some form of sexual harassment during their undergraduate or graduate careers; and many will suffer severe physical, emotional, and professional damage as a result. Female staff and faculty are equally vulnerable, and the incidence rate is as alarmingly high. College communities cannot afford to ignore this issue or treat it as a minor concern; they have a clear and compelling moral, legal, and academic obligation to make this issue a prime focus of education and to provide the means for taking appropriate action when it has occurred.

Hunter has been fortunate in having a strong, explicit City University policy against sexual harassment and a very effective Panel to lead the educational efforts and implementation of that policy. The Panel has represented our conviction that sexual harassment requires broad and representative community action. The particular circumstances of other colleges and universities may indicate alternative means to address this common concern. This resource manual provides information that can be adapted to the needs of any campus including the federal statutes that mandate the appropriate action to be taken in order to end sexual harassment; the results of research on its incidence and traumatic effects; alternative means to assist those who have been victimized and to take action against their harassers; and specific suggestions for educating the college community, conducting interviews, and establishing organizational networks.

In the experience of Hunter's Panel—as they have met with concerned members of other colleges' faculty and administration—and in my own experience, a successful effort to combat sexual harassment requires the strong public commitment of the institution's president and chief administrative officers. This year, members of Hunter's Panel will undertake a college-wide educational campaign,

beginning with workshops led by Professors Barickman and Paludi
for the administrative officers and department chairs of the college,
and culminating in a "Sexual Harassment Awareness Week." Unless
colleges and university systems recognize through major efforts at
education and remedy, the damage done to their communities by
sexual harassment, countless students, faculty, and staff members
will continue to be victimized each year; and the effort to provide an
environment that nurtures learning and academic accomplishment
will be substantially undermined.

Paul LeClerc

Introduction

We are the current coordinators of the Sexual Harassment Panel at Hunter. Michele is a developmental psychologist who specializes in women's achievement and career pathways; at present she is investigating sexual and gender harassment of undergraduate and graduate women of color. She is the editor of *Ivory power: Sexual harassment on campus* (Albany: SUNY Press, 1990). Richard is co-author (with Susan MacDonald and Myra Stark) of *Corrupt relations* (New York: Columbia University Press, 1982), a study of sexuality and gender in nineteenth-century fiction. He is an associate professor of English at Hunter, where he helped establish the Panel in 1982.

The Hunter Panel has three main functions:

1. To conduct research on academic sexual harassment and to publicize the results for the academic community;

2. To educate the academic community about the definitions, incidence, and dimensions of sexual harassment;

3. To investigate informal and formal complaints of sexual harassment made by individuals of the Hunter community against other members of the college.

The Panel is appointed by the president of Hunter, currently Paul LeClerc. (Donna Shalala was president when the Panel was first formed.) The results of our investigations and recommendations for corrective action are made to President LeClerc and to the vice-president for student affairs (also the dean of students at Hunter), Sylvia Fishman. However, the Panel is independent of the administrative structures of the President's Office and the Office of Student Services.

Members of the Panel currently include three psychologists specializing in research on academic and workplace sexual harassment who have conducted research at Hunter. Their findings have been used for our educational and investigative work. This research has included data on the incidence of sexual harassment of women of color and re-entry women, data on peer harassment, and assessments of attitudes and attributions about academic sexual harassment.

In the fall of 1989, the *Chronicle of Higher Education* published an article by Debra Blum on the unusual nature of our Panel. (Most campuses have an ombudsperson, affirmative action officer, or college-appointed investigator who deals with sexual harassment complaints.) The response to Ms. Blum's article has been quite favorable. As a result, colleges and universities across the country have asked us to share our research findings, educational material, and methods for dealing with this problem.

We hope that you will benefit from using this manual, and would like to hear from you about these resources. Your comments about topics covered and/or omitted, illustrations, and presentations would be most helpful for subsequent editions of this manual. Please write us at the following address:

Richard Barickman and Michele Paludi
Hunter College Sexual Harassment Panel
Hunter College
695 Park Avenue
New York, NY 10021

A great many individuals deserve recognition for their participation in our work. We would like to express our appreciation to them: Debra Blum, Meg Bond, Robie Cagnina, Janet Cyril, Connie Engleman, Sylvia Fishman, Louise Fitzgerald, Howard Gadlin, Lisa Goldstein, Marilyn Haring-Hildore, Myra Hindus, Linda Howard, Paul LeClerc, Jean Levitan, Paula Levitt, Father William McConnville, Karen Nolan, Anne Nelson, Robert Nordvall, Richard Koppenal, Helen Remick, Sue Perry, Paula Rothenberg, Bernice Sandler, Pamela Schneider, Sandra Shullman, Arnold Speert, Gazella Summitt, K. C. Wagner, Ann Chapman Waldrop, and Bill Warters.

We also offer our sincere thanks to the members of the Hunter College Sexual Harassment Panel for 1989–1991: Michael Carrera, Vernell Daniels, Darlene DeFour, Lisa Goldstein, Donald Grimm, Dorothy O. Helly, Helen Jacobson, Kathryn Katzman, Susan Lees,

Mary Lefkarites, Andrea Marino, Lorraine McKenney, Sally Pola-koff, Rosemarie Roberts, Pamela Schneider, Rose Ann Schill, Ruth Smallberg, Neal Tolchin, Sue Rosenberg Zalk, Dottie Waters, Stuart Weiss.

We especially want to thank Bernice Sandler, director of the Project on the Status and Education of Women, Association of American Colleges, for her dedication to the field of sex equity in education, for her support and encouragement, and for collaborating with us in helping to make sexual harassment a public concern rather than a hidden issue.

Definitions and Incidence
of Academic and Workplace
Sexual Harassment

Overview

What is sexual harassment?
Do you feel that the following experiences illustrate forms of sexual harassment?

> Dr. P. gave me the creeps. Whenever we took a test, I'd look up from my paper, and there he would be, staring at my top or my legs. I quit wearing skirts to that class because I was so uncomfortable around him. I felt like I was some kind of freak in a zoo.

> Dr. Y. asked me if I wished to share a motel room with him at meetings to be held in the spring. Following our return from these meetings (at which I did not share a motel room with him), he began criticizing my work, suggesting that there was something wrong with my master's thesis data, suggesting that my experimental groups would not replicate, etc. (Dziech & Weiner, 1984)

> I was discussing my work in a public setting when a professor cut me off and asked if I had freckles all over my body.

> He (the teaching assistant) kept saying, "Don't worry about the grade," and, "You know we'll settle everything out of class."

> I see male colleagues and professors chum it up and hear all the talk about making the old boy network operate for women, so I thought nothing of accepting an invitation from a . . . professor to attend a gathering at his house. Other graduate students were present. . . . The professor made a fool out of himself pursuing me (it took me a while to catch on) and then blurted, "You know I

1

want to sleep with you; I have a great deal of influence. Now, of course I don't want to force you into anything, but I'm sure you're going to be sensible about this." I fled.

Playboy centerfolds were used as Anatomy teaching slides. . . . In slides, lectures, teaching aids and even in our own student note service, we found that nurses were presented as sexy, bitchy, or bossy but never as professional health care workers.

The financial officer made it clear that I could get the money I needed if I slept with him. (U.S. Department of Education, Office for Civil Rights, pamphlet, *Sexual harassment: It's not academic*

Definitions of sexual harassment are important because they educate the campus community and workplace and promote discussion and conscientious evaluation of these experiences. They are also crucial to the process of helping those who have been harassed because most individuals do not identify what has happened to them as sexual harassment. In reference to academic sexual harassment, Crocker (1983) suggests, "The effectiveness of any definition will depend not only on the grievance procedure that enforces it, but also the commitment of the university administration and faculty to creating a truly nondiscriminatory environment for all students" (p. 707). MacKinnon (1979) notes that "it is not surprising . . . that women would not complain of an experience for which there has been no name. Until 1976, lacking a term to express it, sexual harassment was literally unspeakable, which made a generalized, shared, and social definition of it inaccessible" (p. 27). She further states that "the unnamed should not be taken for the nonexistent" (p. 28). (Current research indicates that two million women currently enrolled in undergraduate and graduate schools will experience some form of sexual harassment during their careers as students.)

Legal Definitions

Two major types of definitions of sexual harassment have appeared in the legal, psychological, and educational literature. The first type includes legal and regulatory constructions and theoretical statements. Fitzgerald (1990) refers to these definitions as a priori definitions, theoretical in nature, which consist of a general statement describing the nature of the behavior. Table 1.1. presents a

Table 1.1
A Priori Definitions of Sexual Harassment

Equal Employment Opportunity Commission

> Unwelcome sexual advances, requests for sexual favors, and other verbal or physical conduct of a sexual nature constitute sexual harassment when (1) submission to such conduct is made either emplicitly or implicitly a term or condition of an individual's employment; (2) submission to, or rejection of, such conduct by an individual is used as the basis for employment decisions affecting such individual; or (3) such conduct has the purpose or effect of substantially interfering with an individual's work performance or creating an intimidating, hostile, or offensive working environment.

National Advisory Council on Women's Educational Programs

> Academic sexual harassment is the use of authority to emphasize the sexuality or sexual identity of the student in a manner which prevents or impairs that student's full enjoyment of educational benefits, climate, or opportunities.

MacKinnon (1979)

> Sexual harassment . . . refers to the unwanted imposition of sexual requirements in the context of a relationship of unequal power. Central to the concept is the use of power derived from one social sphere to lever benefits or impose deprivations in another. . . . When one is sexual, the other material, the cumulative sanction is particularly potent.

Office for Civil Rights, U.S. Department of Education

> Sexual harassment consists of verbal or physical conduct of a sexual nature, imposed on the basis of sex, by an employee or agent of a recipient of federal funds that denies, limits, provides different, or conditions the provision of aid, benefits, services, or treatment protected under Title IX.

priori definitions from the Equal Employment Opportunity Commission (EEOC), the Office for Civil Rights (OCR) of the Department of Education, the National Advisory Council on Women's Educational Programs, and MacKinnon (1979).

Workplace and academic sexual harassment is clearly prohibited as a form of sexual discrimination, under both Title IX of the 1972 Education amendments and, for employees, Title VII of the 1964

Civil Rights Act. According to the EEOC's definition, the last condition—the creation of "an intimidating, hostile, or offensive working or learning environment"—is significant, because it covers the most pervasive form of sexual harassment, the form most often defended on the grounds of "academic freedom." In a 1986 decision, *Meritor Savings Bank v. Vinson* (see table 1.2), the Supreme Court unani-

Table 1.2
Summary of Legal Cases in Sexual Harassment

Tomkins v. Public Service Electric & Gas Co.
    United States Court of Appeals
    Third Circuit, 1977
    568 F.2d 1044
    Aldisert, Circuit Judge

Miller v. Bank of America
    United States Court of Appeals
    Ninth Circuit, 1979
    600 F.2d 2111
    Duniway, Circuit Judge

Bundy v. Jackson
    United States Court of Appeals for the District of Columbia
    1981
    641 F.2d 934
    Wright, Chief Judge

Henson v. City of Dundee
    United States Court of Appeals
    Eleventh Circuit, 1982
    682 F.2d 897
    Vance, Circuit Judge

Meritor Savings Bank v. Vinson
    Supreme Court of the United States
    1986
    477 U.S., 106 S.Ct., 91 L.Ed.2d 49
    Justice Rehnquist delivered the opinion of the Court

Alexander v. Yale University
    United States Court of Appeals
    Second Circuit, 1980
    631 F.2d 178
    Lumbard, Circuit Judge

mously affirmed that "sexual harassment claims are not limited simply to those for which a tangible job benefit is withheld ["quid pro quo" sexual harassment], but also include those in which the complainant is subjected to an offensive, discriminatory work environment ("hostile environment" sexual harassment)" (Bennett-Alexander, 1987, p. 65). In doing so, the Court explicitly adopted the EEOC's guidelines, which have been extended to the academic community—especially to students, who are not covered by the statutes governing employer/employee relations—by the OCR. These guidelines thus have a regulating force supported by the U.S. Department of Education that is crucial to the effort to curtail the widespread sexual harassment now afflicting our colleges and universities.

In response to the decision in *Vinson*, and in the spirit of this effort, the American Council on Education issued the following statement to all its members in December 1986:

> Although the *Vinson* decision applies specifically to employment, it is prudent to examine the case and its implications for the campus setting. This provides an opportunity to renew institutional commitment to eliminating sexual harassment, or to develop an institution-wide program to address the problem. . . .
>
> The educational mission of a college or university is to foster an open learning and working environment. The ethical obligation to provide an environment that is free from sexual harassment and from the fear that it may occur is implicit. The entire collegiate community suffers when sexual harassment is allowed to pervade the academic atmosphere through neglect, the lack of a policy prohibiting it, or the lack of educational programs designed to clarify appropriate professional behavior on campus and to promote understanding of what constitutes sexual harassment. Each institution has the obligation, for moral as well as legal reasons, to develop policies, procedures, and programs that protect students and employees from sexual harassment and to establish an environment in which such unacceptable behavior will not be tolerated.

Empirical Definitions

The second type of definition summarized by Fitzgerald (1990), is developed empirically, by investigating what various groups of individuals perceive sexual harassment to be under different circumstances (see table 1.3).

Table 1.3
Empirical Definitions of Sexual Harassment

Till (1980)

Generalized sexist remarks
Inappropriate and offensive, but essentially sanction-free sexual advances
Solicitation of sexual activity or other sex-linked activity by promise of
   reward
Coercion of sexual activity by threat of punishment
Sexual crimes and misdemeanors

Fitzgerald et al. (1988)

Gender harassment
Seductive behavior
Sexual bribery
Sexual coercion
Sexual imposition

The most useful definition is the one offered by Fitzgerald et al. (1988). They view sexual harassment along a continuum, with gender harassment on one end, and sexual imposition on the other (see table 1.4). These levels correlate with legal definitions of sexual harassment. *Gender harassment* consists of generalized sexist remarks and behavior not designed to elicit sexual cooperation, but rather to convey insulting, degrading, or sexist attitudes about women or

Table 1.4
Levels of Sexual Harassment

Gender Harassment	Seductive Behavior	Sexual Bribery	Sexual Coercion	Sexual Assault

Gender Harassment: Generalized sexist statements and behavior that convey insulting, degrading, and/or sexist attitudes

Seductive Behavior: Unwanted, inappropriate, and offensive physical or verbal sexual advances

Sexual Bribery: Solicitation of sexual activity or other sex-linked behavior by promise of reward

Sexual Coercion: Coercion of sexual activity or other sex-linked behavior by threat of punishment

Sexual Assault: Assault and/or rape

about lesbians and gays. *Seductive behavior* is unwanted, inappropriate, and offensive sexual advances. *Sexual bribery* is the solicitation of sexual activity or other sex-linked behavior by threat of punishment, *sexual coercion* is the coercion of sexual activity by threat of punishment, and *sexual imposition* includes gross sexual imposition, assault, and rape.

Based on her research with the measurement of sexual harassment, Fitzgerald (1990) offers the following definition:

> Sexual harassment consists of the sexualization of an instrumental relationship through the introduction or imposition of sexist or sexual remarks, requests, or requirements, in the context of a formal power differential. Harassment can also occur where no such formal power differential exists, if the behavior is unwanted by, or offensive to, the woman. Instances of harassment can be classified into the following general categories: gender harassment, seductive behavior, solicitation of sexual activity by promise of reward or threat of punishment, and sexual imposition or assault.

This definition has several advantages. First, it has an empirical component. Second, the nature and levels of sexual harassment are drawn from the experiences of women who have been so victimized. Third, the concept of intent is not addressed. It is, rather, the power differential and/or the woman's reaction that are considered to be the critical variables. As Fitzgerald (1990) states,

> When a formal power differential exists, all sexist or sexual behavior is seen as harassment, since the woman is not considered to be in a position to object, resist, or give fully free consent; when no such differential exists, it is the recipient's experience and perception of the behavior as offensive that constitutes the defining factor. (p. 24)

We would add that the pervasive abuse and contempt for women and lesbians and gays in our culture underlie this form of harassment.

There is one issue that this definition does not specifically address: consensual relationships. The definition by Fitzgerald implies that consensual relationships are not possible within the context of unequal power and are inappropriate. As Zalk, Paludi, and Dederich (1990) point out with respect to academic sexual harassment:

> It is not just the distorted aggrandisement by the student or the greater store of knowledge that is granted the professor that frames

the student's vision before and during the initial phases of the affair. The bottom line in the relationship is *POWER.* The faculty member has it and the student does not. As intertwined as the faculty-student roles may be, and as much as one must exist for the other to exist, they are not equal collaborators. The student does not negotiate indeed, has nothing to negotiate with. There are no exceptions to this, and students know this.

Crocker (1983) argued that it is important to offer definitions of academic sexual harassment since

> they can educate the community and promote discussion and conscientious evaluation of behavior and experience. Students learn that certain experiences are officially recognized as wrong and punishable; professors are put on notice about behaviors that constitute sexual harassment; and administrators shape their understanding of the problem in a way that directs their actions on student inquiries and complaints. (p. 697)

Thus, a definition of academic sexual harassment sets the climate for the campus's response (as well as the workplace's response) to these incidents.

Mead has called for "new taboos" against sexual harassment.

> What should we—what can we—do about sexual harassment on the job? . . . As I see it, it isn't more laws that we need now, but new taboos. . . .
>
> When we examine how any society works, it becomes clear that it is precisely the basic taboos—the deeply and intensely felt prohibitions against "unthinkable" behavior—that keep the social system in balance. . . . The complaints, the legal remedies, and the support institutions developed by women are all part of the response to the new conception of women's rights. But I believe we need something much more pervasive, a climate of opinion that includes men as well as women, and that will affect not only adult relations and behavior on the job but also the expectations about the adult world that guide our children's progress into that world. What we need, in fact, are new taboos, that are appropriate to the new society we are struggling to create—taboos that will operate within the work setting as once they operated within the household. Neither men nor women should expect that sex can be used either to victimize women who need to keep their jobs, or to keep women from advancement or to help men advance their own careers. (as quoted in Dziech & Weiner, 1984, p. 184)

Women Organized against Sexual Harassment (1981) at the University of California, Berkeley, proposed four requirements that have been used as guides by colleges and universities in writing their policy statements concerning sexual harassment. Guidelines must (1) acknowledge sexual harassment as sex discrimination, not as isolated instances of misconduct; (2) refer to a full range of harassment from subtle innuendos to assault; (3) refer to ways in which the context of open and mutual academic exchange is polluted by harassment; and (4) refer to harassment as the imposition of sexual advances by a person in a position of authority. Crocker (1983) pointed out that to be effective, these requirements must (1) recognize the legal basis for university action and place the problem in a social context; (2) recognize the need for, and value of, specific examples that suggest the range of behaviors and experiences considered sexual harassment; (3) recognize the importance of sexual harassment for the integrity of the academy; and (4) recognize that sexual harassment occurs between people who have unequal power.

Defining academic sexual harassment from organizational and sociocultural power perspectives has been interpreted by some colleges and universities as including consensual relationships. Zacker and Paludi (1989) reported that some campuses have adopted a policy statement that includes information about consensual relationships (see table 1.5). Including consensual relationships as part of the definition of academic sexual harassment has been met with great resistance (Sandler, 1988; Zacker & Paludi, 1989). Men are much less likely than women to include consensual relationships in their definition of sexual harassment (Kenig & Ryan, 1986; Fitzgerald et al., 1988). Additional information about attitudes and perceptions of sexual harassment is discussed in chapter 3.

Incidence of Sexual Harassment in the Workplace and in College/University Settings

Table 1.6 summarizes the incidence rates of sexual harassment in the academic and workplace settings. As can be seen from this data, its occurrence in U.S. schools and business is widespread. Dziech and Weiner (1984) have reported that 30% of all undergraduate women suffer sexual harassment from at least one of their instructors during their college careers. When definitions of sexual harassment include sexist remarks and other forms of "gender harassment," the incidence rate in undergraduate populations nears

Table 1.5
Policy Statements from Universities that
Deal with Consensual Relationships

University of Iowa's Policy on Sexual Harassment

Amorous relationships between faculty members and students occurring outside the instructional context may lead to difficulties. Particularly when the faculty member and student are in the same academic unit or in units that are academically allied, relationships that the parties view as consensual may appear to others to be exploitative. Further, in such situations (and others that cannot be anticipated), the faculty member may face serious conflicts of interest and should be careful to distance himself or herself from any decisions that may reward or penalize the student involved. A faculty member who fails to withdraw from participation in activities or decisions that may reward or penalize a student with whom the faculty member has or has had an amorous relationship will be deemed to have violated his or her ethical obligation to the student, to other students, to colleagues, and to the University.

Harvard University's Policy on Sexual Harassment

Amorous relationships that might be appropriate in other circumstances are always wrong when they occur between any teacher or officer of the University and any student for whom he or she has a professional responsibility. Further, such relationships may have the effect of undermining the atmosphere of trust on which the educational process depends. Implicit in the idea of professionalism is the recognition by those in positions of authority that in their relationships with students there is always an element of power. It is incumbent upon those with authority not to abuse, nor to seem to abuse, the power with which they are entrusted. . . . Even when both parties have consented to the development of such a relationship, it is the officer or instructor who, by virtue of his or her special responsibility, will be held accountable for unprofessional behavior. Because graduate student teaching fellows, tutors, and undergraduate assistants may be less accustomed than faculty members to thinking of themselves as holding professional responsibilities, they would be wise to exercise special care in their relationships with students whom they instruct or evaluate. . . . Relationships between officers and students are always fundamentally asymmetric in nature.

70% (Lott, Reilly, & Howard, 1982; Adams, Kottke, & Padgitt, 1983). These percentages translate into millions of students in our college

Table 1.6
Summary of Research on the Incidence of Sexual Harassment

Adams, Kottke, and Padgitt (1983)

> 13% of women students surveyed, reported they had avoided taking a class or working with certain professors because of the risk of being subjected to sexual advances; 17% received verbal sexual advances, 13.6% received sexual invitations; 6.4% had been subjected to physical advances; 2% received direct sexual assault

Chronicle of Higher Education Report of Harvard University (1983)

> 15% of the graduate students and 12% of the undergraduate students who had been sexually harassed by their professors changed their major or educational program because of the harassment

Wilson and Kraus (1983)

> 8.9% of the female undergraduates in their study had been pinched, touched, or patted to the point of personal discomfort

Bailey and Richards (1985)

> 12.7% of 246 graduate women surveyed reported that they had been sexually harassed; 21% had not enrolled in a course to avoid such behavior; 11.3% tried to report the behavior, 2.6% dropped a course because of it; 15.9% reported being directly assaulted

Bond (1988)

> 75% of 229 faculty experienced jokes with sexual themes during their graduate training; 68.9% were subjected to sexist comments demeaning to women; 57.8% of the women reported experiencing sexist remarks about their clothing, body, or sexual activities; 12.2% had unwanted intercourse, breast, or genital stimulation

Gutek (1985)

> 53.1% of private sector workers surveyed reported being fired, not being promoted, not given raises, all because of refusal to comply with requests for sexual relationships

system who are harassed each year. (According to the Chronicle of Higher Education, there were 6,835,900 women enrolled in undergraduate and graduate programs in 1987. Thirty percent of this figure equals more than 2,000,000 students who experience sexual

Table 1.6—*Continued*

Cornell University (Reported in Farley, 1978)

> 70% of 195 women workers reported sexual harassment and 56% of these women reported physical harassment

National Merit Systems Protection Board (1981)

> 42% of 23,000 women and men surveyed—the largest survey ever taken of workplace sexual harassment—experienced sexual harassment

harassment. When gender harassment in included, the number is 4,785,000.) The incidence rate for women graduate students and faculty is even higher (Bailey & Richards, 1985; Bond, 1988). Though there are few studies focusing on the harassment of nonfaculty employees in the college/university system, there is no reason to suppose that the harassment of college staff is any less than the 50%-rate reported for employees of various other public and private institutions (Fitzgerald et al., 1988).

While both women and men can be harassed, women make up the majority of victims. This is true for incidents of peer harassment as well. *Peer harassment* is the term used to describe the sexual harassment of women by their male colleagues—women students harassed by male students, for example; women faculty harassed by male faculty; and gay and lesbian students harassed by other students. Peer harassment includes all of the levels of sexual harassment: gender harassment, seductive behavior, sexual bribery, sexual coercion, and sexual imposition (see table 1.7).

Peer harassment occurs at all types of academic and business settings—large and small, private and public. Peer harassment creates an environment that makes education and work less than equal for women and men. There have been a few major surveys done on peer harassment. For example, in 1986, Cornell University surveyed its women students and found that 78% of those responding had experienced one or more forms of peer harassment, including sexist comments and unwelcome attention. While most of these experiences involved individual men, a substantial percentage involved groups of men, termed *group harassment*. MIT also conducted a study of peer harassment and reported that 92% of the women were harassed by male students. At the University of Rhode Island, 70% of the women reported instances of peer harassment.

Table 1.7
Illustrations of Peer Harassment

A group of men regularly sit at a table facing a cafeteria line. As women go through the line, the men loudly discuss the women's sexual attributes and hold up signs with numbers from 1 to 10, "rating" each woman. As a result, many women skip meals or avoid the cafeteria.

Sexist posters and pictures appear in places where women will see them.

A fraternity pledge approaches a young woman he has never met and bites her on the breast—a practice called "sharking."

A particular shop [class's] predominantly male population designated one shop day as "National Sexual Harassment Day," in honor of their only female student. They gave her nonstop harassment throughout the day, and found it to be so successful (the female student [dropped the course]) that they later held a "National Sexual Harassment Week."

Source: Project on the Status and Education of Women.

These surveys also indicate that the most serious forms of peer harassment involve groups of men. When men outnumber women, as in fraternity houses, stadiums, and parties, group harassment is especially likely to occur. Examples of group harassment include:

"scoping," which involves rating women's attractiveness on a scale from 1 to 10;

yelling, whistling, and shouting obscenities at women who walk by fraternity houses or other campus sites;

intimidating a woman by surrounding her, demanding that she expose her breasts, and not allowing her to leave until she complies:

creating a disturbance outside of women's residence halls;

vandalizing sororites;

harassing women who support women's rights;

date rape.

Research has indicated that while any individual is likely to be sexually harassed, women tend to experience this more often than others. Sandler (1988) and DeFour (1990) have indicated that on many campuses ethnic minority women are victims because of the stereotypes and myths that portray them as sexually active, exotic, and erotic. There is thus an interface of racism and sexism in some elements of sexual harassment.

In addition, physically challenged women experience a considerable amount of psychological victimization when reporting sexual harassment due to stereotypes about their sexuality and attractiveness. Lesbians and gays have been the victims of gender harassment and other forms of sexual harassment because of homophobic attitudes. Individuals who support women's studies programs and are feminists are also often targeted.

Most of the current incidence rates of sexual harassment have been obtained from research using the Sexual Experiences Questionnaire (Fitzgerald & Shullman, 1985). (see table 1.8.) As can be seen from this table, all of the items in the survey are written in behavioral terms and take the form of: "Have you ever been in a situation where a professor or instructor . . . ?" The term *sexual harassment* does not appear in any item until the end ("Have you ever been sexually harassed by a professor or instructor?"). Items represent the five levels of sexual harassment derived from research: gender harassment, seductive behavior, sexual bribery, sexual coercion, and sexual assault. For each item, individuals are asked to circle the response most closely describing their own experiences: "Never," "Once," and "More than Once." If individuals indicate that the behavior has happened either once or more than once, they are further instructed to identify the sex of the faculty member: "Male," "Female," or "Both Male and Female." Information concerning the reliability and validity of this instrument and parallel forms for employees may be found in Fitzgerald et al. (1988).

Research with this instrument has indicated that women are more likely to be the recipients of sexual harassment than men. In nearly all cases, the perpetrators are men. Furthermore, while the majority of women in undergraduate and graduate training programs as well as in the workplace indicate that they have experienced behaviors that legally constitute sexual harassment, they fail to recognize and label their experiences as such. For example, Fitzgerald et al. (1988) found that although at one university nearly 28% of the women administrators reported that they had been propositioned by male co-workers, only 5% of the women felt that they had been sexually harassed.

Fitzgerald and Weitzman (1990) reported that of the 235 male faculty members they surveyed (using a modified form of the Sexual

Table 1.8
Sexual Experiences Questionnaire

On the following pages, you will find a series of questions requesting information about many different kinds of sexual experiences that occur on a college campus. We are principally interested in sexual behavior between faculty and students, so most of the questions are about this type of situation. Please note that we are interested in your experiences as a college student, either graduate or undergraduate, *whether or not* these experiences occurred at your current campus or somewhere else.

Please answer as honestly as you can. Remember that all information collected in a research study is *completely confidential,* and your privacy is completely protected. Thank you for your assistance with this important project.

Demographic Data

1. Sex: Male _____ Female _____

2. Race: White _____ Black _____ Hispanic-American _____

   Asian-American _____

   Other (Please specify) _____

3. Age: _____

4. Year: Freshman _____

   Sophomore _____

   Junior _____

   Senior _____

   Graduate Student _____

5. Major: _____

Instructions: For each item, please circle the number which most closely describes your own experience. If you circle 2 or 3, please say whether the person involved was a man or a woman (or both, if it happened more than once) by circling M, F, or B.

	Never	Once	More than Once	Sex
1–1. Have you ever been in a situation where a professor or instructor habitually told suggestive stories or offensive jokes?	1	2	3	M F B

Table 1.8—*Continued*

	Never	Once	More than Once	Sex
1–2. Have you ever been in a situation where a professor made crudely sexual remarks, either publicly in class, or to you privately?	1	2	3	M F B
1–3. Have you ever been in a situation where a professor or instructor made seductive remarks about your appearance, body, or sexual activities?	1	2	3	M F B
1–4. Have you ever been in a situation where a professor was staring, leering, or ogling you in a way that was inappropriate, or that made you uncomfortable?	1	2	3	M F B
1–5. Other than in classes on human sexuality or similar topics, have you ever been in a class where the instructor used sexist or suggestive teaching materials (e.g., pictures, stories, pornography)?	1	2	3	M F B
1–6. Have you ever been in a situation where a professor treated you "differently" because you were a male or female (i.e., favored one sex or the other)?	1	2	3	M F B
1–7. Have you ever been in a situation where the instructor made sexist remarks (e.g., suggesting that traditionally masculine fields like engineering are inappropriate for women, or that there must be something "wrong" with men who want to be nurses)?	1	2	3	M F B

Table 1.8—*Continued*

	Never	Once	More than Once	Sex
2–1. Have you ever been in a situation where a professor or instructor made unwanted attempts to draw you into a discussion of personal of sexual matters (e.g., attempted to discuss or comment on your sex life)?	1	2	3	M F B
2–2. Have you ever been in a situation where a professor or instructor engaged in what you considered seductive behavior toward you (e.g., made flattering or suggestive remarks, asked you for a date, suggested that you "get together" for a drink, offered to give you a backrub)?	1	2	3	M F B
2–3. Have you ever been in a situation where you received unwanted sexual attention from a professor or instructor?	1	2	3	M F B
2–4. Have you ever been in a situation where a professor or instructor attempted to establish a romantic sexual relationship with you?	1	2	3	M F B
2–5. Has a professor or instructor ever "propositioned" you?	1	2	3	M F B
3–1. Have you ever felt that you were being subtly bribed with some sort of *reward* (e.g., good grades or preferential treatment) to engage in sexual behavior with a professor or instructor?	1	2	3	M F B

Table 1.8—*Continued*

	Never	Once	More than Once	Sex
3–2. Have you ever been in a situation where a professor or instructor *directly* offered you some sort of reward for being sexually cooperative?	1	2	3	M F B
3–3. Have you ever engaged in sexual behavior you did not want to engage in because of such promises or rewards?	1	2	3	M F B
3–4. Have you ever been in a situation where you actually were rewarded by a professor or instructor for being socially or sexually *cooperative* (e.g., going out to dinner, having drinks, establishing a sexual relationship)?	1	2	3	M F B
4–1. Have you ever felt that you were being subtly threatened with some sort of "punishment" for not being sexually cooperative with a professor or instructor (e.g., lowering your grade, failing an exam, etc.)?	1	2	3	M F B
4–2. Have you ever been *directly* threatened or pressured to engage in sexual activity by threats of punishment or retaliation?	1	2	3	M F B
4–3. Have you ever been in a situation where you actually experienced some negative consequences for refusing to engage in sexual activity with a professor or instructor?	1	2	3	M F B

Table 1.8—*Continued*

	Never	Once	More than Once	Sex
4–4. Have you ever engaged in a sexual behavior that you did not want to engage in because of such threats or fear of punishment?	1	2	3	M F B
5–1. Have you ever been in a situation where a professor or instructor made unwanted attempts to touch or fondle you (e.g., stroking your leg or neck, touching your breast and so forth)?	1	2	3	M F B
5–2. Have you ever been in a situation where a professor or instructor made *forceful* attempts to touch, fondle, kiss, or grab you?	1	2	3	M F B
5–3. Have you ever been in a situation where a professor or instructor committed indecent exposure (i.e., displayed their genitals to you)?	1	2	3	M F B
5–4. Have you ever been in a situation where a professor made unwanted attempts to have sexual intercourse with you that resulted in your crying, pleading, or physically struggling?	1	2	3	M F B
5–5. Have you ever been in a situation where a professor or instructor attempted to force you to touch their genitals?	1	2	3	M F B

Table 1.8—*Continued*

	Never	Once	More than Once	Sex
5–6. Have you ever been in a situation where a professor or instructor used force (squeezing your wrist, twisting your arms, holding you down, etc.) to have intercourse with you?	1	2	3	M F B
5–7. Have you ever been sexually harassed by a professor or instructor?	1	2	3	M F B
5–8. Have you ever been raped by a professor or instructor?	1	2	3	M F B

If you have experienced *any* of the situations/behaviors described on this survey, please answer the following questions:

A. Have you ever dropped a course to avoid such behavior?   Yes   No

B. Have you ever avoided or not enrolled in a course to avoid such behavior?   Yes   No

C. Have you ever tried to report such behavior?   Yes   No

D. If so, what happened? If not, why not?

Did you ever experience any of these situations when you were in high school? _____ Yes _____ No

If so, please describe:

This is your space. Please use it to give reactions to the questionnaire, to describe any related experiences you would like to share, or simply to tell us anything you like concerning yourself, your experiences, or this research. Use the back of the sheet if you like.

Thank You!

Experiences Questionnaire); the majority reported engaging in behavior that meets the legal definition of sexual harassment, yet only one man reported that he had sexually harassed a student. Fitzgerald and Weitzman further concluded that faculty who sexually harass students are not distinguishable from their colleagues with respect to age, marital status, academic rank, or academic discipline. Sexual harassers tend to be repeat offenders, however.

Different conclusions were drawn from research conducted by the United States Merit Systems Protection Board (1981). Surveys were sent to more than 23,000 women and men civilian employees of the Executive Branch of the U.S. government; a response rate of 85% was achieved. Results indicated that women in the federal workforce are likely to be harassed by a male co-worker who is married, older than the woman, and white, and who harassed other women as well. Results also indicated that when the harassment involved attempted rape or sexual assault, supervisors were more likely to be the harasser of the women, than were peers.

Do Women Harass?

Research in academic sexual harassment suggests that women professors are highly unlikely to date or initiate sexual relationships with male or female students (Fitzgerald & Weitzman, 1990). In the workplace as in the academic environment, women are much less likely to hold the organizational power that would permit them to offer sexual rewards and/or punishments. As Fitzgerald and Weitzman conclude:

> Although it is theoretically possible for women to harass men, it is, in practice, an extremely rare event. This is due both to the women's relative lack of formal power, and the socialization that stigmatizes the sexually aggressive woman. Reports by male subjects of sexual overtures by women co-workers not only do not constitute harassment in any formal sense, but must also be evaluated in light of data suggesting that men are likely to interpret relatively innocuous behavior as invitations to sexual contact. (p. 66)

These issues concerning perceptions about sexuality, sexual harassment, and power are discussed further in chapter 4.

Summary

Both formal academic research and the growing experience of those taking action against harassment in the campus community and workplace indicate that it is one of the most pervasive and least recognized forms of abuse in our society. In the 1981 study by the National Merit Systems Protection Board, of over 23,000 employees, 42% reported harassment. Numerous studies have produced similar (and higher) rates for students in undergraduate and graduate institutions. Based on enrollment figures for 1987, reported in the *Chronicle of Higher Education*, over 2,000,000 undergraduate and graduate women students will be singled out for harassment during their academic careers. When gender harassment is added to the continuum of sexual harassment, the number nearly doubles.

Sexual harassment is clearly prohibited as a form of discrimination under Title IX of the 1972 Education amendments and Title VII of the 1964 Civil Rights Act. Despite these federal statutes, only a few colleges, businesses, and agencies have implemented active programs in order to educate their constituents and to investigate complaints. Because both harassers and the harassed usually fail to identify the abuse as sexual harassment, most incidents go unreported even when a mechanism for redress exists. Those seeking to reduce the incidence of sexual harassment in campus environments have found that an intensive educational campaign is a precondition for success.

Because of power structures within the workplace and the academy and because of deeply embedded cultural biases, women are overwhelmingly the targets of sexual harassment. And even though no "profile" of a typical harasser has been developed in research, nearly all harassers are male. Identification of sexual harassment as a "women's issue," however, rather than as a pervasive pattern of abuse that contaminates a whole community, only creates another impediment to its identification and elimination.

Sample References on Workplace Sexual Harassment

Bennett-Alexander, D. D. (1987). The Supreme Court finally speaks on the issue of sexual harassment—what did it say? *Women's Rights Law Reporter, 10,* 65–78.

Farley, L. (1978). *Sexual shakedown: The sexual harassment of women on the job.* New York: McGraw-Hill.

Goodwin, M. P., Roscoe, B., Rose, M., & Repp, S. E. (1989). Sexual harassment: Experiences of university employees. *Initiatives, 52,* 25–33.

Gruber, J., & Bjorn, L. (1982). Blue-collar blues: The sexual harassment of women autoworkers. *Work and Occupations: An International Sociological Journal, 9,* 271–98.

Gutek, B. (1985). *Sex and the workplace: The impact of sexual behavior and harassment on women, men, and organizations.* San Francisco: Jossey-Bass.

Gutek, B., & Dunwoody, V. (1987). Understanding sex in the workplace. *Women and Work, 2,* 249–69.

Hair, S. (1987). Sexual harassment, subtle or overt gnaws at productivity. *Employee Assistance Quarterly, 3,* 67–70.

Hopkins, C., & Johnson, D. A. (1982). Sexual harassment in the workplace. *Journal of College Placement, 42,* 30–35.

Lafontaine, E., & Tleadeau, L. (1986). The frequency, sources, and correlates of sexual harassment among women in traditional male occupations. *Sex Roles, 15,* 433–42.

Littler-Bishop, S., Seidler-Feller, D., & Opaluch, R. (1982). Sexual harassment in the workplace as a function of initiatator's status: The case of airline personnel. *The Journal of Social Issues, 38,* 137–48.

Loy, P., & Stewart, L. (1984). The extent and effects of the sexual harassment of working women. *Sociological Focus, 17,* 31–43.

Maypole, D. (1986). Sexual harassment of social workers at work: Injustice within? *Social Work, 31,* 29–34.

Maypole, D., & Skaine, R. (1983). Sexual harassment in the workplace. *Social Work, 28,* 385–90.

MacKinnon, C. (1979). *Sexual harassment of working women: A case of sex discrimination.* New Haven, Conn.: Yale University Press.

Petersen, D., & Massengill, D. (1982). Sexual harassment: A growing problem in the workplace. *Personnel Administrator, 27,* 79–89.

Popovich, P. (1988). Sexual harassment in organizations. *Employee Responsibilities and Rights Journal, 1,* 273–82.

United States Merit Systems Protection Board (1981). *Sexual harassment in the federal workplace: Is it a problem?* Washington, D.C.: U.S. Government Printing Office.

Sample References on Academic Sexual Harassment

Adams, J., Kottke, J., & Padgitt, J. (1983). Sexual harassment of university students. *Journal of College Student Personnel, 24,* 484–90.

Association of American Colleges (1988). *Peer harassment: Hassles for women on campus.* Washington, D.C.: Project on the Status and Education of Women.

Bailey, N., & Richards, M. (1985, August). *Tarnishing the ivory tower: Sexual harassment in graduate training programs.* Paper presented at the Annual Meeting of the American Psychological Association, Los Angeles, CA.

Betts, N, & Newman, G. (1982). Defining the issues: Sexual harassment in college and university life. *Contemporary Education, 54,* 48–52.

Bond, M. (1988). Division 27 Sexual harassment survey: Definition, impact, and environmental context. *The Community Psychologist, 21,* 7–10.

Cammaert, L. (1985). How widespread is sexual harassment on campus? Special Issue: Women in groups and aggression against women. *International Journal of Women's Studies, 8,* 388–97.

Coleman, M. (1987). A study of sexual harassment of female students in academia. *Dissertation Abstracts International, 47,* 2815.

Connolly, W. B. Jr., & Marshall, A. B. (1989). Sexual harassment of university or college students by faculty members. *Journal of College and University Law, 15,* 381–403.

Crocker, P. (1983). An analysis of university definitions of sexual harassment. *Signs, 8,* 696–707.

DeFour, D. C. (1990). The interface of racism and sexism on college campuses. In M. A. Paludi (Ed.), *Ivory power: Sexual harassment on campus.* Albany: SUNY Press.

Dziech, B., & Weiner, L. (1984). *The lecherous professor.* Boston: Beacon Press.

Fitzgerald, L. F. (1990). Sexual harassment: The definition and measurement of a construct. In M. A. Paludi (Ed.), *Ivory power: Sexual harassment on campus.* Albany: SUNY Press.

Fitzgerald, L. F., & Shullman, S. (1985, August). The development and validation of an objectively scored measure of sexual harassment. Paper presented at the Annual Meeting of the American Psychological Association, Los Angeles.

Fitzgerald, L., Shullman, S., Bailey, N., Richards, M., Swecker, J., Gold, Y., Ormerod, M., & Weitzman, L. (1988). The incidence and dimensions of sexual harassment in academia and the workplace. *Journal of Vocational Behavior, 32*, 152–75.

Fitzgerald, L. F., & Weitzman, L. (1990). Men who harass: Speculation and data. In M. A. Paludi (Ed.), *Ivory power: Sexual harassment on campus.* Albany: SUNY Press.

Franklin, P., Moglin, H., Zatling-Boring, P., & Angress, R. (1981). *Sexual and gender harassment in the academy.* New York: Modern Language Association.

Gartland, P. (Ed.) (1983). Sexual harassment on campus. *Journal of the National Association of Women Deans, Administrators and Counselors, 46*, 3–50.

Ingulli, E. D. (1987). Sexual harassment in education. *Rutgers Law Journal, 18*, 281–342.

Kenig, S., & Ryan, J. (1986). Sex differences in levels of tolerance and attribution of blame for sexual harassment on a university campus. *Sex Roles, 15*, 535–49.

Lott, B. (1982). Sexual assault and harassment: A campus community case study. *Signs, 8*, 296–319.

Lott, B., Reilly, M. E., & Howard D. R. (1982). Sexual assault and harassment: A campus community case study. *Signs, 8*, 296–319.

Mazer, D. B., & Percival, E. F. (1989). Students' experiences of sexual harassment at a small university. *Sex Roles, 20*, 1–22.

Reilly, M., Lott, B., & Gallogly, S. (1986). Sexual harassment of university students. *Sex Roles, 15*, 333–58.

Robertson, C. (1988). Campus harassment: Sexual harassment policies and procedures at institutions of higher learning. *Signs, 13*, 792–812.

Sandler, B. (1981). Sexual harassment: A hidden problem. *Educational Record, 62*, 52–57.

Sandler, B. (1988, April). Sexual harassment: A new issue for institutions, or these are the times that try men's souls. Paper presented at the Conference on Sexual Harassment on Campus, New York.

Singer, T. L. (1989). Sexual harassment in graduate schools of social work: Provocative dilemmas. *Journal of Social Work Education, 25,* 68–76.

Schneider, B. (1987). Graduate women, sexual harassment, and university policy. *Journal of Higher Education, 58,* 46–65.

Small, M. J. (1989). The guardians of Heloise? Sexual harassment in higher education. *Educational Record, 70,* 42–45.

Somers, A. (1982). Sexual harassment in academe: Legal issues and definitions. *The Journal of Social Issues, 38,* 23–32.

Till, F. (1980). *Sexual harassment: A report on the sexual harassment of students.* Washington, D.C.: National Advisory Council on Women's Educational Programs.

Wilson, K. R., & Krauss, L. A. (1983). Sexual harassment in the university. *Journal of College Student Personnel, 24,* 219–24.

Zacker, M., & Paludi, M. A. (1989). Educational programs for academic sexual harassment. Unpublished manuscript, Hunter College.

Zalk, S. R., Paludi, M. A., & Dederich, J. (1990). Women students' assessment of consensual relationships with their professors. Manuscript in preparation, Hunter College.

CHAPTER 2

In Their Own Voices: Responses from Individuals Who Have Experienced Sexual Harassment and Supportive Techniques for Dealing with Victims of Sexual Harassment

Overview

What is the impact of sexual harassment?

The consequences of being sexually harassed devastates one's physical well-being, emotional health, and vocational development. Dziech and Weiner (1984) conclude that it often "forces a student to forfeit work, research, educational comfort, or even career. Professors withhold legitimate opportunities from those who resist, or students withdraw rather than pay certain prices" (p. 10). Women who have been harassed typically change their major, job assignment, educational program, or career goals as a result. In addition, women have reported emotional and physical reactions to being harassed, including depression, insomnia, headaches, helplessness, and decreased motivation. Sexual harassment in the workplace frequently occurs in a social context in which women experience physical hardship, loss of income, administrative neglect, and isolation.

All of these experiences contribute to emotional and physical stress reactions. In recent years, the label "Sexual Harassment Trauma Syndrome" (Shullman 1989) has been applied to the effects of harassment on the physical, emotional, interpersonal, and career aspects of women's lives. Research has indicated that depending on the severity of the harassment, between 21% and 82% of all women report that their emotional and/or physical condition deteriorated as a result (Koss 1990). Furthermore, like victims of rape who go to court, harassment victims experience a second victimization when they attempt to deal with the situation through legal and/or institutional means. Stereotypes about sexual harassment and women's victimization blame women for the harassment (MacKinnon 1979; see chap. 3). These stereotypes center around the myths that sexual harassment is a form of seduction, that women secretly want to be sexually harassed, and that women do not tell the truth.

Individual responses to academic and workplace harassment vary, of course, as a function of the victim's personal style, the severity of the harassment, and the availability of social support. However, postvictimization generalized stress responses experienced by the majority of women victims can be summarized (see table 2.1). It is not surprising, considering that the continuum of harassment includes sexual assault, that the responses of women who have been harassed often parallel the responses of women who have been raped.

Research has indicated that women victims suffer long-term aftereffects. Quina (1990), for example, analyzes these responses according to common features of the victimization experience for women: sexual harassment (1) causes severe trauma; (2) violates trust, especially when the harasser is in a position of authority, for example, a professor or boss; and (3) causes secondary losses, including the lack of support and comfort from family and friends, and retaliation when charges are filed (e.g., being fired or receiving a failing course grade).

Furthermore, when the sexual harassment occurs in an academic setting, the stress reactions experienced by women often occur gradually, since faculty may be able to manipulate their authority over women students in subtle ways (Rabinowitz 1990). As Koss (1990) points out; "Experiencing sexual harassment transforms women into victims and changes their lives. It is inevitable that once victimized, at minimum, one can never again feel quite as invulnerable" (p. 37).

As Dziech and Weiner (1984) point out, "To understand sexual harassment, one must listen to the accounts of its victims . . . nothing can capture its meaning and truth better than the voices of women who have endured it" (p. 89) (see table 2.2). These responses are taken from the Project on the Status and Education of Women (1978) and from Till (1980).

Common reactions to being sexually harassed, as indicated by the responses in table 2.2 include feeling

1. confused and/or embarrassed
   Have I misinterpreted the situation?

Table 2.1
Sexual Harassment Trauma Syndrome

Emotional Reactions

> Anxiety, shock, denial
> Anger, fear, frustration
> Insecurity, betrayal, embarrassment
> Confusion, self-consciousness
> Shame, powerlessness
> Guilt, isolation

Physical Reactions

> Headaches
> Sleep disturbances
> Lethargy
> Gastrointestinal distress
> Hypervigilance
> Dermatological reactions
> Weight fluctuations
> Nightmares
> Phobias, panic reactions
> Genitourinary distress
> Respiratory problems
> Substance abuse

Changes in Self-Perception

> Negative self-concept/self-esteem
> Lack of competency
> Lack of control
> Isolation
> Hopelessness
> Powerlessness

Social, Interpersonal Relatedness, and Sexual Effects

> Withdrawal
> Fear of new people, situations
> Lack of trust
> Lack of focus
> Self-preoccupation
> Changes in social network patterns
> Negative attitudes and behavior in sexual relationships
> Potential sexual disorders associated with stress and trauma
> Changes in dress or physical appearance

Table 2.1—*Continued*

Career Effects

    Changes in study and work habits
    Loss of job or promotion
    Unfavorable performance evaluations
    Drop in academic or work performance because of stress
    Lower grades as punishment for reporting sexual harassment or
      for noncompliance with sexual advances
    Absenteeism
    Withdrawal from work and school
    Changes in career goals

    Am I overreacting?
    Have I done something to lead him or her on?

2. helpless
    No one is going to believe me.
    It's his or her word against mine.
    If I complain, it will make matters worse.

3. angry and/or insulted
    I'm being cheated out of an education.
    Why isn't any one doing something about his or her behavior?

4. worried
    I'll never get a good recommendation from him or her if I don't go along with him or her.
    All the other professors will know if I file a complaint.
    Everyone will say I'm too sensitive.

As Koss (1990) recommends:

It is very important that the counselor keep roles straight. . . . The clinician is not a judge and doesn't have to be concerned with whether sexual harassment as legally defined has occurred. Likewise, the clinician is not an attorney. Clinicians should only help clients with their options, not advise them on their civil rights. . . . Also, clinicians must make clients aware that making a claim of psychological damages will require them to waive their right to confidentiality in the sessions and the treating therapist may be called to trial to present an assessment of the client. (p. 43)

Table 2.2
In Their Own Voices:
Accounts from Women Who Have Experienced Sexual Harassment

*I was ashamed, thought it was my fault, and was worried that the school would take action against me—for "unearned" grades—if they found out about it.

*This happened years ago, and you are the first person I've been able to discuss it with in all that time. He's still at—, and probably still doing it.

*I'm afraid to tell anyone here about it, and I'm just hoping to get through the year so I can leave.

*Who was going to believe me? I was an undergraduate student and he was a famous professor. It was an unreal situation.

*It may . . . be unnecessary to bring to your attention a fact which you probably suspect to be the case on my campus: those persons with the authority to take responsible action are themselves men.

*The dean told me that she would check into it, but it's been months and I haven't heard anything. Meanwhile, he goes on just like before.

*We were informed that there was nothing the school could do. Both the counselor and the student acted as consenting adults off the campus ground.

*One professor in my major was constantly making comments about "how cute I was" or "how serious" or "how motivated I seemed to be" after class or while I was studying in the library. Needless to say, I felt very uncomfortable and started wearing old jeans to his classes.

*I . . . became quite skilled at glancing down department hallways to make sure he wasn't there before venturing forth, and pretending not to see him when we did cross paths. The whole experience has left me quite mistrustful of faculty in general and I still feel some trepidation when visiting the department.

*The impact of this isolated incident on me has been enormous. It has changed my way of relating to the program. I used to think it could be a place of learning, mentoring, work, and fun. Now, although there are still people there whom I trust and learn from, I am angry and insecure every time I'm in that building. I have heard that this professor has propositioned at least two other students, and I am silently furious. I've said nothing about this except to my husband. . . .

*This incident has unfortunately left me feeling disillusioned and wary of male professors. I know it isn't right to generalize like that, but I can't help the uneasy feeling.

Table 2.2—*Continued*

*I do not believe other profs in the department would do anything against him—in fact, I think they all know what's going on. . . . To get rid of him as a chairperson would cause me considerable stress and reprogramming. I feel harassed and foolish for having believed his interest was in my program.

*Later on, Dr. _____ took me aside and explained to me how women rarely make good field geologists. This, he maintained, was due to their difficulty in perceiving things in three dimensions. He contended that when figuring out GRE, SAT, and ACT (etc.) scores, the "educators" take this inherent deficiency into account.

*One physics professor gave his students a lecture on the effects of outer space on humans. His example consisted of crude drawings of a shapely woman supine in a vessel; the effects of [a] vacuum were demonstrated by changes in the size of her "boobs." This man—a "mature" adult—told the story with all of the sniggering, head-hanging, and red-facedness I might have expected from an adolescent.

Source: Till, 1980; Project on the Status and Education of Women, 1978.

Shullman (1989) has reported that understanding the psychological impact of sexual harassment is related to the victim's perceptions and cognitive appraisals of her experiences. The victimization process activates negative self-images. Frequently, victims view themselves as needy, frightened, weak, and out of control. The victimization forces women "to realize that their 'cognitive baggage'— the assumptions and expectations that they have held about themselves and their world—have been severely challenged and may no longer be viable" (Janoff-Bulman & Frieze 1983, 3).

For the victimization to be resolved, shattered beliefs must be reformulated so as to assimilate the experience of sexual harassment. Taylor (1983) has termed this process "cognitive readjustment." Successful cognitive re-adjustment of beliefs includes a discovered ability to cope, learn, adapt, and become self-reliant. Cognitive re-adjustment produces a greater sense of self-confidence, maturity, honesty, and sense of strength (Finkel 1975). Taylor (1983) pointed out that the cognitive re-adjustment process involves three themes: (1) the search for meaning—"Why did this happen to me?" (2) the attempt to gain mastery and control over one's life—"How can I prevent further harassment?" and (3) the attempt to promote self-enhancement—"Now that I have experienced sexual harassment, who am I?"

Table 2.3
Supportive Techniques for Working with Victims
of Sexual Harassment

1. *Validation of Feelings:* "I didn't make it up."
Emotional support that legitimates victim status may help individual resist self-devaluation

2. *Search for Meaning:* "Why me?"
Discussion of gender inequity may help individual realize that sexual harassment is an abuse of power

3. *Expression of Anger*
Provision of a safe forum for the expression of anger may help individual contain feelings in a classroom/workplace and preserve effective performance as much as possible

4. *Monitor Damage*
Seek documentation of health problems and difficulties as a form of legal protection

5. *Provision for Mourning Losses*
A first step for rebuilding new beliefs, new lives, and new support systems

6. *Offer Hope*
Careers and relationships can be rebuilt

Source. Adapted from Koss (1990).

Koss (1990) recommends techniques for assisting women in their cognitive re-appraisal of sexual harassment (see table 2.3). Quina (1990) also recommends the following for working with women victims of sexual harassment:

1. Cast the experience as a sexual assault and recognize its effects.

2. Find others with similar experiences and share stories.

3. Recognize the personal losses of sexual harassment and allow for a grieving process.

4. Join or form a feminist network and support group to prevent future traumata for others as well as for oneself.

It is helpful for clinicians working with these victims to use the following guidelines (Hamilton et al., 1989):

1. The woman actually has experienced discrimination.

2. She probably has an adequate or better work (and/or) education history.

3. She probably has reacted in some way to the discrimination, which has already been brought to her attention.

4. If she has complained, there has been retaliation.

A list or organizations dealing with sexual harassment is presented in table 2.4.

Shullman (1989) and Lundberg-Love (1989) recommend the use of bibliotherapy as an educational approach to assisting with cognitive re-adjustment (see table 2.5).

All of the techniques suggested here enlighten women about their options and help them make more informed choices about dealing with sexual harassment and its effects. These techniques are useful in empowering women, who typically feel vulnerable and out of control because of the victimization process.

Summary

Women who have been harassed typically experience physical and emotional damage, now recognized as the Sexual Harassment Trauma Syndrome paralleling reactions of rape victims. They also suffer from a severe negative impact, which affects their educational and career advancement. Many lose jobs or promotions, change academic programs, or mistrust educational opportunities that they previously found appealing and promising.

Because sexual harassment is not publicly acknowledged as a major form of abuse, women often respond to it with confusion, doubt, self-blame, and a desire to flee from the situation rather than report it. Again, the urge to alter *their* behavior, appearance, or situation, also commonly characterizes women who have been raped. At this time many more people (rape victims, physicians, lawyers, counselors, and police personnel) have an understanding of this dimension of the trauma of rape, incest, and sexual molestation of children. Sadly, sexual harassment, which causes similar trauma, is often treated as a minor problem or even as a joke. Hearing the actual responses of those who have been harassed dispels this facile and erroneous assumption. In a striking parallel to sexual harass-

Table 2.4
List of Organizations Concerned with Sexual Harassment

Additional information may be obtained by contacting the Project on the Status and Education of Women of the Association of American Colleges, 1818 R St., NW, Washington, DC 20009.

Alliance against Sexual Coercion
P.O. Box 1
Cambridge, MA 02139

American Association of University Professors
1 Dupont Circle
Washington, DC 20036

American Council on Education
Office of Women in Higher Education
Washington, DC 20036

American Psychological Association
1200 17th St. NW
Washington, DC 20036

Cleveland Women Working
1258 Euclid Avenue
Cleveland, OH 44115

Equal Employment Opportunity Commission
2401 E St., NW
Washington, DC 20507

Institute for Women and Work
Cornell University
15 East 26th St.
New York, NY 10010

National Association for Women Deans, Administrators,
   and Counselors
1625 1st St., NW
Washington, DC 20006

New York Women against Rape
666 Broadway
New York, NY 10012

Table 2.4—*Continued*

9 to 5
YWCA
140 Clarendon St.
Boston, MA 02116

Stop Sexual Abuse of Students
Chicago Public Education Project
American Friends Service Committee
407 South Dearborn St.
Chicago, IL 60605

U.S. Commission on Civil Rights
New England Office
55 Summer St.
Boston, MA 02110

U.S. Department of Education
Office for Civil Rights
Washington, DC 20202

Vocations for Social Change
353 Broadway
Cambridge, MA 02139

ment, recent studies have shown that the great majority of women who have been raped by acquaintances are unlikely to identify the assault as rape and are likely to blame themselves. (A study at the University of Massachusetts found that 13% of undergraduate women had been raped by acquaintances; another 10% had been subjected to sexual assault or attempted rape; but only 3% had reported the attacks.) Before education and remedial action can significantly change the climate of misunderstanding and indifference that allows sexual harassment to occur, we must listen to the voices of those who have been traumatized.

Table 2.5
List of Readings on Sexual Harassment for
Bibliotherapeutic Purposes

Dziech, B., & Weiner, L. (1984). *The lecherous professor.* Boston: Beacon Press.

Gutek, B. (1985). *Sex and the workplace: The impact of sexual behavior and harassment on women, men, and organizations.* San Francisco, Calif.: Jossey-Bass.

Hughes, J., & Sandler, B. (1986). *In case of sexual harassment: A guide for women students: We hope it doesn't happen to you but if it does . . .* Washington, D.C.: Project on the Status and Education of Women.

MacKinnon, C. (1979). *Sexual harassment of working women: A case of sex discrimination.* New Haven, Conn.: Yale University Press.

Omillian, S. (1987). *Sexual harassment in employment.* Wilmette, Ill.: Callaghan & Co.

Paludi, M. A. (Ed.) (1990). *Ivory power: Sexual harassment in the academy.* Albany: SUNY Press.

Additional readings may be found by consulting the following periodicals:
   Women's Studies Abstracts
   Studies on Women Abstracts
   Catalyst Resource on the Workforce and Women
   Educational Resources Information Center
   Sociological Abstracts
   Psychological Abstracts
   Legal Resources Index
   Index of Economic Articles
   National Newspaper Index
   Magazine Index
   Alternative Press Index

References

Crull, P. (1982). Stress effects of sexual harassment on the job: Implications for counseling. *American Journal of Orthopsychiatry, 52,* 539–44.

Dziech, B. W., & Weiner, L. (1984). *The lecherous professor.* Boston: Beacon Press.

Finkel, J. J. (1975). Stress, traumas, and trauma resolution. *American Journal of Community Psychology, 3,* 173–78.

Glass, B. (1988). Workplace harassment and the victimization of women. *Women's Studies International Forum, 11,* 55–67.

Gosselin, H. (1984). Sexual harassment on the job: Psychological, social, and economic repercussions. *Canada's Mental Health, 32,* 21–24.

Gruber, J., & Bjorn, L. (1986). Women's responses to sexual harassment: An analysis of sociocultural, organizational, and personal resource models. *Social Science Quarterly, 67,* 814–26.

Hamilton, J. A., Alagna, S. W., King, L. S., & Lloyd, C. (1989). The emotional consequences of gender-based abuse in the workplace: New counseling programs for sex discrimination. *Women and Therapy.*

Honstead, M. L. (1988). Correlates of coping methods of sexually harassed college students. *Dissertation Abstracts International, 48,* (8–A), 7512.

Janoff-Bulman, R., & Frieze, I. H. (1983). A theoretical perspective for understanding reactions to victimization. *Journal of Social Issues, 39,* 1–17.

Koss, M. P. (1990). Changed lives: The psychological impact of sexual harassment. In M. A. Paludi (Ed.), *Ivory power: Sexual harassment on campus.* Albany: SUNY Press.

Lundberg-Love, P. (1989, August). Clinical interventions with victims of sexual harassment. Paper presented at the American Psychological Association, New Orleans, La.

MacKinnon, C. (1979). *Sexual harassment of working women: A case of sex discrimination.* New Haven, Conn.: Yale University Press.

Project on the Status and Education of Women (1978). *Sexual harassment: A hidden issue.* Washington, D.C.: Association of American Colleges.

Quina, K. (1990). The victimization of women. In M. A. Paludi (Ed.), *Ivory power: Sexual harassment on campus.* Albany: SUNY Press.

Rabinowitz, V. C. (1990). Coping with sexual harassment. In M. A. Paludi (Ed.), *Ivory power: Sexual harassment on campus.* Albany: SUNY Press.

Shullman, S. (1989), March). Sexual harassment: Therapeutic issues and interventions. Paper presented at the Association for Women in Psychology, Newport, R.I.

Taylor, S. E. (1983). Adjustment to threatening events: A theory of cognitive adaptation. *American Psychologist, 38,* 1161–73.

Thomann, D. A., & Weiner, R. L. (1987). Physical and psychological causality as determinants of culpability in sexual harassment cases. *Sex Roles, 17,* 573–91.

Till, F. (1980). *Sexual harassment: A report on the sexual harassment of students.* Washington, D.C.: National Advisory Council on Women's Education Programs.

*Dealing with Academic and Workplace Sexual
Harassment: Individual, Institutional,
and Legal Remedies*

Overview

How can one deal with sexual harassment?
Three main strategies for dealing with sexual harassment can be
summarized as follows: individual, institutional, and legal.

Individual Strategy

Writing a Letter to the Harasser

Mary Rowe, the affirmative action officer at MIT, suggests that
writing a letter to the harasser frequently stops the harassment. She
recommends that the letter consist of three sections: (1) a factual account of what happened, (2) a description of the way the writer feels
about the events that occurred, and (3) a statement of what the
writer wants to happen next (see table 3.1). Rowe also recommends
the following:

1. Deliver the letter in person or by registered or certified mail.

2. Do not send copies of this letter to the press or college administrators.

3. Keep at least one copy of the letter.

4. Don't discuss the letter with the harasser if you do not
want to.

Table 3.1
Writing a Letter to the Harasser

Factual Account of What Happened

In this section, it is recommended that the factual description of the events that took place be nonevaluative. This section should be as detailed as possible, including dates, places, people present, and a description of the incidents. For example, "On Wednesday, May 24 during your office hours (2:00–4:00 P.M.), I came to discuss the grade you gave me on my term paper (B–). During the course of our discussion you patted my thigh and hugged me twice."

Description of Feelings about Incident

In this section, the writer needs to document feelings about the events described in the first section. For example, "My stomach turned to knots during my visit with you in your office hours"; "I am afraid to come to class because I don't want you to ever touch me or look at me the way you did."

What Writer Wants to Happen Next

In this section the writer needs to express what she or he would like to happen next. For example, "I don't ever want you to touch me or hug me again."

Writing a letter to the harasser can be a successful individual strategy because

1. it helps the victim gain a sense of control over the situation;

2. it breaks a pattern of silence the victim may have kept out of fear of retaliation and/or disbelief;

3. it maintains confidentiality;

4. it provides harassers with information about the way their behavior is being interpreted by another individual;

5. it most likely avoids formal charges and a public confrontation;

6. it suggests that the victim is willing to take action to stop the harassment.

Institutional Strategies

The following questions need to be addressed when dealing with harassment in the college/university or workplace:

1. Does the institution have a policy dealing with sexual harassment? If so, become familiar with this policy and publicize it through student newspapers, faculty and student handbooks, pamphlets, and brochures. Is there an informal procedure to help resolve complaints prior to bringing formal charges?

2. Individuals may want to rehearse what they want to say about their experiences with a friend. They may also want to take a friend with them when they discuss their experiences with their representative. The representative of the college, business, or agency should be asked the following questions:
*Will the complainant's name be used?
*Will the harasser be notified about the charges immediately?
*When and how will the complainant be notified about the way the investigation is progressing?

3. It is not necessary to have had repeated instances of sexual harassment in order to bring charges against an individual.

4. There are usually deadlines involved in institutional procedures for handling complaints.

5. A diary of all experiences with the harasser, witnesses present, copies of letters, et cetera, should be maintained.

Using an institutional strategy can be intimidating—these procedures take time and involve considerable embarrassment and stress for those who have been harassed. Individuals may want to find out whether others in their institution have used these procedures and how they were treated in the process. Also, it is important to ask who conducts the investigation—a panel? Ombudsperson? Individuals may want to investigate whether there is anyone at their institution who can assist them in preparing their cases—for example, is there a women's center on campus?

We recommend the use of panels to investigate complaints of academic sexual harassment. Because this most commonly occurs in a context of institutional power, those who have been victimized are often, understandably, reluctant to use the ordinary channels for re-

Table 3.2
Description of the Hunter College Sexual Harassment Panel

Panel members are appointed by the president of Hunter College, and the Panel reports to both the president and the vice-president for student affairs, but it is independent of the administrative structures of the President's office and the Office of Student Services.

The fact that the Panel guarantees that all procedures will be confidential and further guarantees that the individual bringing the complaint will decide whether to make a formal complaint also encourages individuals to contact Panel members to discuss a problem. Unless individuals feel that they will have these protections, victims will seldom report the sexual harassment they have experienced. Research findings fully support this conclusion. Obviously, individual complaints cannot be resolved and the pervasive injury done to the academic and workplace community by sexual harassment cannot be remedied unless complaints are actually reported.

The Panel has prepared extensive educational materials for new Panel members and regularly engages in training sessions, attends conferences, consults with experts at other campuses, and so forth. The Panel now includes two counselors and three psychologists whose research specializations include the area of sexual harassment.

solving complaints. This is especially true because of the humiliating and disorienting impact of sexual harassment, where the victim may experience the sort of self-doubt, self-blame, and sense of degradation common to victims of rape, incest, and battering (see chap. 2). It is important, therefore, that the means of hearing and resolving complaints of sexual harassment should be distinct from the regular administrative hierarchies. A description of Hunter's Panel is presented in table 3.2.

To promote the effective and equitable resolution of problems involving sexual harassment, it seems necessary to have

1. an explicit policy adopted by the college or university or workplace in compliance with the provision of Titles VII and IX, applicable to all units of the system. Such a policy allows the university and college to uphold and enforce its policies against sexual harassment within its own community (including such severe penalties as loss of pay or position or tenure) without requiring victimized individuals to undertake the laborious, protracted, and costly process of seeking redress from the courts under Titles VII and IX.

2. one body of individuals, delegated by, and responsible to, the president of the college or company, who are specially knowl-

edgeable about the nature of sexual harassment and trained to deal with both complaints and those accused of harassment fairly, sensitively, and confidentially.

3. a body composed of faculty, staff, and students so that the whole college community is represented. Under Hunter's policies, a person may contact any member of the Panel for initial, informal discussion. In order to make access to the Panel as easy and as comfortable as possible, its membership reflects the diversity of the college community, in terms of sex, sexual orientation, academic programs and ranks, and racial and ethnic background. Research has indicated, and the Panel's experience has confirmed, that many feel more comfortable contacting someone they identify with as a peer, so that the more diverse the composition of the Panel in terms of status, sex, race, and so forth, the more access it provides the community it serves.

4. common definitions of sexual harassment and common procedures for resolving conflicts applied equitably throughout the institution, regardless of the status of the complainant or the person complained against. Without a common procedure, inequities can easily occur in the effort to protect individuals' rights under Titles VII and IX.

Remick et al. (1990) have offered suggestions concerning the characteristics of a "good" investigator of complaints of sexual harassment. (1) Investigators must conduct the investigations and write recommendations and reports in clear, objective language, be fair and candid, and not have their personal feelings interfere with effectiveness; (2) investigators must be sensitive to the hierarchy in the academic or workplace setting; and (3) investigators must be sensitive to the issues involved in sexual harassment, including sexuality, power, and anger toward women. Investigators must maintain a distance from all individuals involved in the investigations so that they can make an informed judgment about the complaint and be upheld as objective by hearing officers, judges, college presidents, et cetera. Remick et al. also recommend an interview team consisting of a woman and a man when doing investigations.

> Outside of the interview situation, each can use the other for occasional reality checks and for support. "Mixed" teams do not seem to interfere with reporting; the interviewee simply tends to make eye contact with the same sex person while answering sensitive

questions. For the female complainant, the team approach offers
a "safer" environment than talking about sex to a strange man.
(p. 91)

Copies of policy statements and procedures from two colleges
are presented in table 3.3. Additional policy statements may be
found in *Sexual harassment on campus: A legal compendium.*

Howard Gadlin, the ombudsperson at the University of Massachusetts, Amherst, recommends mediation as an effective way for
resolving complaints of sexual harassment (see table 3.4).

Legal Strategies

Civil Suit

Victims may consider suing a person who is sexually harassing
them. An attorney might take their case on a percentage basis.
However, civil suits are time-consuming and there have been instances of countersuits.

Criminal Suit

When victims have experienced sexual assault they may consider bringing a criminal suit against their harasser. For further information about this strategy, an attorney recommended by the
women's center or women's studies faculty at their local campus
should be consulted.

State Laws

Victims should inquire as to whether there is any applicable
state law against sexual harassment. Some state civil rights laws prohibit sex discrimination. In addition, inquiries about state laws may
be made by contacting the following:

    state Civil Rights Commission
    state Women's Commission
    state Fair Employment Practices Commission
    local office of the Office for Civil Rights under the Department of
        Education
    local chapter of the National Organization for Women
    local chapter of the American Civil Liberties Union
    state Bar Association

Table 3.3
Examples of Policy Statements and Procedures Dealing
with Sexual Harassment

Gettysburg College

GRIEVANCE PROCEDURES CONCERNING SEXUAL DISCRIMINATION,
DISCRIMINATION ON THE BASIS OF HANDICAP, SEXUAL
HARASSMENT, AND SOME COMPLAINTS ABOUT TERMS
AND CONDITIONS OF EMPLOYMENT

I. Who May Use These Grievance Procedures

The Grievance Procedures below are for all employees and students at Gettysburg College who have a complaint about actions of an employee of the College. These procedures do not apply to applicants for admission or employment at the College. The person presenting a grievance is called "the grievant" below. The person whose actions are the basis of the grievance is called "the respondent." The term "days" in this document means calendar days.

II. What Categories of Grievances Are Not Covered by These Procedures

Gettysburg College has additional Grievance Procedures for the following situations. Grievants with a complaint that falls under these other procedures should refer to them.

    A. Dismissal of a Faculty Member for Cause *(Faculty Handbook).*
    B. Non-Reappointment of a Non-Tenured Faculty Member *(Faculty Handbook).*
    C. Rights of Students Under the Rights and Responsibilities of Students *(Student Handbook).*

III. What Can be the Subject of a Grievance Under These Procedures

The procedures below apply to grievances concerning:

    A. Alleged Sex Discrimination Under Title IX of the Education Amendments of 1972.
    B. Alleged Discrimination on the Basis of Personal Handicap Under Section 504 of the Rehabilitation Act of 1973.
    C. Complaints of Sexual Harassment Committed by an Employee of the College.
    D. Complaints Reasonably Related to Terms and Conditions of Employment of an Employee of the College (except for complaints covered under the Grievance Procedures listed in II above).

Table 3.3—*Continued*

Grievances concerning salary or promotion or termination of employment which might fall under the provisions of these Grievance Procedures are only covered when it is reasonably alleged that the action complained of was a result of discrimination based on race, color, sex, national origin, personal handicap, or age.

A grievance does not include dissatisfaction with a College policy of general application challenged on the ground that the policy is unfair or inadvisable.

Under these grievance procedures a student may be the grievant but not the respondent. Complaints about the actions of students fall under the jurisdiction of the Dean of Student Life.

IV. Informal Resolution of Complaints

If possible, grievances should be resolved informally between or among the parties involved. If the grievance cannot be informally resolved by these persons, the grievant shall next (within 30 days of the incident that is the basis of the grievance) seek assistance in obtaining an informal resolution by contacting an appropriate person listed below:

A. The Affirmative Action Officer of the College for Grievances Concerning Sexual Discrimination Under Title IX, Racial Discrimination, or Discrimination on the Basis of Personal Handicap Under Section 504 of the Rehabilitation Act of 1973.
B. The Affirmative Action Officer of the College and Others Designated by the President for Complaints of Sexual Harassment by an Employee of the College. The list of persons so designated shall include representatives of the faculty, administration, and support staff. The list of such persons will be widely published on campus and will be available from the Affirmative Action Office, the Office of Student Life, and the Counseling Services Office.
C. The College Grievance Officer for All Other Complaints Under These Grievance Procedures. The College Grievance Officer is an employee of the College to whom the President assigns the additional duties of Grievance Officer on a yearly basis.

The person contacted under this section will work informally with the grievant and the respondent in order to reach a solution satisfactory to all parties. The grievant must submit a written statement to the person contacted that outlines the action or actions that are complained of and the facts that substantiate the complaint. No formal written grievance can be filed under Section V. below until ten days have expired from the date on which one of the persons listed above is contacted to assist in the informal resolution of the grievance. If the grievance cannot be informally resolved within

Table 3.3—*Continued*

ten days to the satisfaction of the grievant and the respondent, the person contacted will provide within seven days (after the end of the ten-day period) to the grievant and respondent a written statement that efforts to resolve the grievance informally were unsuccessful. The ten-day period during which informal resolution is attempted may be extended upon the mutual agreement of the grievant and the respondent.

All proceedings to resolve and formulate a complaint shall be confidential with the understanding that the Affirmative Action Officer will be apprised of such proceedings and that testimony about the informal resolution of these complaints may be heard as part of the hearing process outlined in section V., below.

V. A Formal Resolution of Grievances

A grievant who has received a written statement that the informal grievance resolution efforts were unsuccessful may seek a formal resolution of the grievance. To do this, he or she must file in writing with the College Grievance Officer (within 15 days of the date of the statement that informal resolution efforts were unsuccessful) a formal grievance. This formal grievance shall specify the action or actions that are complained of, the facts that constitute such action, the evidence that will be presented to establish such facts, and the names of witnesses who may testify to present such evidence.

The College Grievance Officer will immediately forward this formal grievance to the respondent and to the Chairperson of the College Grievance Committee. The College Grievance Committee is a committee of four faculty members selected by the Executive Committee, four administrators appointed by the President, and four staff employees appointed by the College Business Manager. It shall select its own chairperson.

When a formal grievance is filed, the Chairperson of the College Grievance Committee shall select a hearing panel of five persons from the Committee to conduct a formal hearing on the grievance. The hearing panel shall have at least two persons from the employee groups (faculty, administration, staff) of each party to the grievance who is an employee of the College. If a student is a party to the grievance, the student may request to the Chairperson of the College Grievance Committee that the hearing panel include one student appointed by the President of the Student Senate. Such student shall be one of the five persons on the hearing panel.

The hearing panel will meet before scheduling a hearing to review the formal grievance and these grievance procedures. The hearing panel may decide on the basis of the written grievance presented to it that the action alleged does not fall within the definition of a grievance under these procedures or that it is of such minimal consequence that a grievance hearing is not merited. In such cases, the panel shall forward this determination within 15 days of the filing of the grievance in writing to the President.

Table 3.3—*Continued*

The hearing panel will schedule a hearing within 20 days of the date of the filing of the grievance with the understanding that complaints filed within 20 days of the end of a semester may be heard in the following semester. At this hearing, the burden of proof will be on the grievant to establish the allegations of the grievance by a preponderance of the evidence. The hearing panel shall select its chairperson. The hearing will not be an open meeting; only the grievant, respondent, and the hearing panel shall select its chairperson. The hearing will not be an open meeting; only the grievant, respondent, and the hearing panel will be present. Witnesses will be present only when their testimony is being taken. There will not be any attorneys present for the parties. The hearing panel will not be bound by strict rules of legal evidence. The panel may receive any evidence of probative value in determining the issues involved. Every possible effort will be made to obtain the most reliable evidence available. All questions relating to the admissability of evidence or other legal matters will be decided by the chairperson of the panel. The parties to the grievance will have the right to present evidence and call witnesses and respond to evidence presented at the hearing. The hearing panel may receive written or oral evidence. It may request an account of the informal efforts to resolve the grievance from the person listed in section IV who assisted in this process. It may call persons to testify before it. It shall compile a summary of the substance of oral and written testimony presented to it. A tape recording of the hearing shall be made and retained for two years, and a transcript shall be prepared free of charge upon the request of the grievant or the respondent.

The hearing panel shall make written findings concerning the allegations of the complaint. A majority vote of the hearing committee shall be required for each finding and recommendation of the group. These findings plus recommendations for resolution of the complaint shall be forwarded within ten days of the hearing to the grievant, the respondent, and to one of the following persons: the Provost if the respondent is a faculty member, the President if the respondent is an administrator, or the Business Manager if the respondent is a staff employee. If the grievant is a student, the Dean of Student Life will also receive a copy of the findings plus recommendations. If the named administrator to whom the findings and recommendations are to be forwarded is a grievant or respondent under the grievance, the findings and recommendations shall be forwarded to the President. The panel has no restrictions upon it as to what it can recommend from a finding that the grievance is not established, to a reprimand, to further proceedings for dismissal of the employee.

The person to whom the report of the hearing panel is forwarded (other than the Dean of Student Life) shall act on the recommendations of the hearing panel within ten days of the receipt of findings and recommendations. These findings and recommendations are not binding upon him or

Table 3.3—Continued

her. His or her decision on the actions to be taken shall be made in writing and submitted to the parties. This person has the power to institute any penalty or determine any resolution of the grievance within the authority of his or her position.

The grievant or the respondent may appeal this decision to the President (or ask for reconsideration of the decision by the President if it was made by him or her) only on the grounds that there was a substantial and prejudicial departure from these procedures in the consideration and the resolution of the grievance or that there is demonstrated new evidence not available to the person making the appeal (appellant) at the time of the hearing and which might have reasonably affected the decision of the hearing panel had it been available. The appellant shall specify the act or acts that constitute such a departure. The President may request that a new hearing panel be constituted to hear the grievance again. In such a case, the grievance procedure will begin again at the formal hearing stage unless the grievant and respondent both agree that informal resolution attempts should first be made. The President's decision on the appeal shall be final.

All proceedings to resolve formally a grievance shall remain confidential among the persons involved and the Affirmative Action Officer of the College.

VI. Grievance Where the President is Respondent

In a case where the President is the respondent in a grievance, the role of the President under these procedures shall be filled by another person chosen by mutual agreement of the President and the grievant.

VII. Report to the College Community

The Affirmative Action Officer should consult with the persons listed in section IV. B. and C. at least yearly and make a report to the College community concerning the number of grievance cases, both formal and informal, that were brought and resolved within the preceding year.

Source: Reprinted by permission, from Robert Nordvall, Gettysburg College.

Hunter College

HUNTER COLLEGE OF THE CITY UNIVERSITY OF NEW YORK
SEXUAL HARASSMENT POLICY STATEMENT AND PROCEDURES
FOR THE SEXUAL HARASSMENT PANEL

INTRODUCTION

Members of an academic community—students, faculty, and staff— must be able to work in an atmosphere of mutual respect and trust. Any

Table 3.3—*Continued*

violation of trust, any form of intimidation or exploitation, damages the institution's educational process by undermining the essential freedoms of inquiry and expression. Students, teachers, and staff must feel personally secure in order for real learning to take place.

As a place of work and study, Hunter College should be free of sexual harassment and all forms of sexual intimidation and exploitation. All students, staff, and faculty must be assured that the college will take action to prevent such misconduct and that anyone who engages in such behavior may be subject to disciplinary procedures.

The Office for Civil Rights of the U.S. Department of Education has issued the following statement on sexual harassment:

> Sexual harassment of students is a real and increasingly visible problem of serious consequence in higher education. A sexual harassment experience can affect all aspects of a student's life: it can threaten a student's emotional well-being, impair academic progress and even inhibit the attainment of career goals.

> Most sexual harassment incidents involve a male harasser and a female victim although there have been several reported cases involving female harassers and male victims as well as same-sex harassment. Other forms of discrimination, such as that based on race, may be combined with an incident of sexual harassment and further compound the severity of its effect and the difficulty of its resolution. Whatever the circumstances, academic institutions must address the problem in order to ensure all students a just and equal learning opportunity.

> Sexual harassment in educational institutions is not simply inappropriate behavior; it is against the law. Sexual harassment of students is a violation of Title IX of the 1972 Education Amendments in that it constitutes differential treatment on the basis of sex. Title IX applies to any educational program or activity which receives Federal funds and protects both employees and students.

POLICY

The CUNY Board of Trustees has adopted an explicit policy prohibiting sexual harassment throughout the university community:

> It is the policy of the City University of New York to prohibit harassment of employees or students on the basis of sex. This policy is related to and is in conformity with the equal opportunity policy of the University to recruit, employ, retain, and promote employees without regard to sex, age, race, color, or creed. Prompt investiga-

Table 3.3—*Continued*

tion of allegations will be made on a confidential basis to ascertain the veracity of complaints, and appropriate corrective action will be taken.

It is a violation of policy for any member of the University community to engage in sexual harassment. It is a violation of policy for any member of the University community to take action against an individual for reporting sexual harassment.

DEFINITION

For the purposes of this policy, sexual harassment is defined as unwelcome sexual advances, requests for sexual favors, and other intimidating verbal or written communications or physical conduct of a sexual nature. This behavior constitutes sexual harassment when:

1. submission to such conduct is made either explicitly or implicitly a term or condition of an individual's employment or academic standing;

2. submission to or rejection of such conduct by an individual is used as the basis for employment or academic decisions affecting that individual;

3. such conduct has the purpose or effect of unreasonably interfering with an individual's work performance or creating an intimidating, hostile, or offensive working or learning environment.*

Sexual harassment takes various forms: generalized sexist remarks or behavior; inappropriate and offensive sexual advances without explicit threats or promises of reward; solicitation of sexual activity or other sex-linked behavior by promise of reward, coercion of sexual activity by threat of punishment; and sexual assaults. All these forms of sexual harassment share certain reprehensible qualities. Those engaged in such behavior distort the relationship of trust that must exist if a college environment is to foster independent, creative and pleasurable learning. They treat individuals in reductive, stereotypic ways that are offensive and demeaning. And they misuse their authority and power to exploit a vulnerable person, contaminating the relations of teacher and student, counselor and client, administrator and teacher, or supervisor and employee.

FUNCTIONS OF THE PANEL

The Panel has three main functions:

1. To help educate the Hunter College community about sexual harassment.

2. To assist in the informal resolution of complaints of sexual harassment brought by employees and students of Hunter College.

---

*These criteria are based on the Equal Employment Opportunity Commissions' Guidelines on Discrimination because of Sex.

Table 3.3—*Continued*

3. When designated by the Vice-President for Student Affairs, to conduct investigations of formal complaints of sexual harassment brought by students against faculty, staff, or other students. The Panel makes recommendations for corrective action to the Vice-President for Student Affairs, who is responsible for reporting her/his findings and recommendations to the President of Hunter College.

PROCEDURES

I. GUIDANCE AND COUNSELING REGARDING SEXUAL HARASSMENT

Any student, staff member, or faculty member is encouraged to discuss incidents of possible sexual harassment with a member of the Panel or with the entire Panel. These discussions will be kept confidential, and no formal complaint is necessary.

A Panel member contacted by a person who may have been subjected to sexual harassment will give advice and guidance on both informal and formal procedures for resolving the problem. The Panel member will give the person a copy of the Sexual Harassment Policy Statement. The Panel member will make a record of the contact, but all information will be kept confidential. No specific circumstances, including the names of the people involved, will be reported to the Panel without the written permission of the person making the complaint.

Anyone who feels subjected to sexual harassment should report the circumstances within 30 days, whether through informal discussion with a Panel member or through a formal complaint, as specified in the CUNY Board of Trustees' guidelines on sexual harassment (January 25, 1982). At any time during the procedures, both the person bringing a complaint and the person against whom the complaint is made may have a representative present in discussions with Panel members.

II. RESOLUTIONS OF INFORMAL COMPLAINTS

A. Any student or employee may discuss an informal complaint with a member of the Panel. If the person who discusses an informal complaint with a member of the Panel is willing to be identified to the Panel, but not to the person against whom the informal complaint is being made, the Panel will make a confidential record of the circumstances and will provide guidance about various ways to resolve the problem or avoid future occurrences.

B. If the person bringing the complaint is willing to be identified to the person against whom the complaint is made and wishes to attempt informal resolution of the problem, the Panel will make a confidential record of the circumstances (signed by the complainant) and suggest and/or undertake appropriate discussions with the people involved.

Table 3.3—*Continued*

C. When a number of people report incidents of sexual harassment that have occurred in a public context (for example, offensive sexual remarks in a classroom lecture) or when the Panel receives repeated complaints from different people that an individual has engaged in other forms of sexual harassment, the Panel may inform the person complained against without revealing the identity of the complainants.

III. FORMAL COMPLAINTS BY STUDENTS

A. Written Statement.

A formal complaint of sexual harassment must include a written statement signed by the complainant specifying the incident(s) of sexual harassment. The statement may be prepared by the complainant or by a Panel member as a record of the complaint. The complaint must be addressed to the Dean of Students/Vice President for Student Affairs, who will then designate the Panel to investigate the complaint, and present its findings and recommendations to the Vice President for Student Affairs.

The Vice President for Student Affairs will report her or his findings to the President with appropriate recommendations.

B. Investigations of formal complaints.

The Panel will investigate formal complaints in the following manner:

1. The Panel member who is first contacted, after initial discussion with the person making the complaint and with that person's written consent, will deliver the complaint to the Panel specifying the individuals involved. The Panel will decide whether the circumstances reported in the complaint warrant an investigation.

2. If the circumstances warrant an investigation, the Panel will inform the person complained against of the name of the person making the complaint as well as of the substance of the complaint. The Panel will assign the investigation to a subcommittee of at least three Panel members. The investigation will be limited to what is necessary to resolve the complaint or make a recommendation. If it appears necessary for the Panel members to speak to any people other than those involved in the complaint, they will do so only after informing the complaining person and the person complained against.

3. The Panel's first priority will be to attempt to resolve the problem through a mutual agreement of the complainant and the person complained against.

4. The Chair of the Subcommittee will be in communication with the complainant until the complaint is resolved. The complainant will be informed of procedures being followed although not of the specific conversations held with the person complained against.

Table 3.3—*Continued*

5. The Panel will resolve complaints expeditiously. To the extent possible, the Panel will complete its investigation and make its recommendations within 60 days from the time the formal investigation is initiated.

6. If a person making a formal complaint asks not to be identified until a later date (for example, until the end of a course), the Panel will decide whether or not to hold the complaint without further action until the date requested.

7. If a formal complaint has been preceded by an informal investigation, the Panel shall decide whether there are sufficient grounds to warrant a formal investigation.

C. Reporting and corrective action.

After an investigation of a complaint the Panel will:

1. resolve the complaint to the satisfaction of the complainant and the person complained against and report its findings and the resolution to the Vice President for Student Affairs; or

2. report its findings with appropriate recommendations for corrective action to the Vice President for Student Affairs; or

3. report to the Vice President for Student Affairs its finding that there is insufficient evidence to support the complaint.

After conducting its investigation, the Panel will make a written report to the Vice President for Student Affairs. If the Panel determines that there has been sexual harassment and corrective action is recommended, the report will specify the circumstances and the action recommended.

IV. FORMAL COMPLAINTS BY EMPLOYEES

A. Employees covered by collective bargaining agreement which include gender discrimination as a ground for grievance shall utilize the grievance procedure provided in their respective agreements.

B. Employees not covered by collective bargaining agreements or covered by an agreement which does not include gender discrimination as a ground for grievance, shall use the procedure in Part III above. The following will also apply for these employees:

1. Formal Complaints are to be addressed to the Sexual Harassment Panel or to a member of the Sexual Harassment Panel.

2. Following an investigation, the Panel will report its findings to the President with appropriate recommendations for corrective action.

3. Following receipt of the report, the President may take such further action as she/he deems necessary, including the initiation of disciplinary proceedings.

Table 3.3—*Continued*

V. RECOMMENDED CORRECTIVE ACTION

The purpose of any recommended corrective action to resolve a complaint will be to correct or to remedy the injury, if any, to the complainant and to prevent further harassment. Recommended action may include: written or verbal reprimand of the harasser; suspension, dismissal, or transfer of the harasser; a change of grade or other academic record for a student who has been the victim of harassment; or other appropriate action.

The Panel has no power to take corrective action beyond making a recommendation to the President or to the Vice President for Student Affairs. Any action to suspend or to dismiss a member of the Instructional Staff is governed by Article 21 of the 1987–1990 Agreement between the City University of New York and the Professional Staff Congress/CUNY or the applicable provision of the successor Agreement in effect at the time of the action. Disciplinary action against employees who are covered by other collective bargaining agreements are governed by the applicable provision of the respective agreement. Disciplinary actions against students are governed by Article 15 of the Bylaws of the Board of Trustees of the City University of New York.

If the complaint involves a grade in a course or if appropriate corrective action involves a change of grade, the Panel may recommend that the Vice President for Student Affairs authorize a change of grade. If the Panel finds no grounds for a change of grade, the student may still use the grade appeal processes established by the Hunter College Senate.

VI. FALSE CHARGES

If the Panel determines that a complaint was made by a student or employee with the knowledge that the facts were false, the Panel shall so notify the Vice President for Student Affairs and may recommend appropriate disciplinary action.

Source: Reprinted by permission, from Paludi, Hunter College.

Additional information concerning legal strategies may be obtained from the following:

Equal Employment Opportunity Commission
2401 E St., NW
Washington, DC 20507

Office for Civil Rights
U.S. Department of Education
330 C St. SW
Washington, DC 20202

Table 3.4
Mediation Principles in Dealing with Complaints
of Sexual Harassment

This material was prepared by Howard Gadlin and is reprinted here with his permission.

MEDIATING SEXUAL HARASSMENT

Introduction—Many sexual harassment policies have provisions permitting informal resolution of sexual harassment complaints. These policies recognize the importance of allowing the harassed person to maintain some control of the process by which the grievance is resolved. Rather than requiring every allegation of sexual harassment to result in a formal hearing on investigation, these policies enable grievants to participate actively in the resolution of their complaints. Often mediation is an effective means for satisfying the grievant while simultaneously educating the harasser. At the University of Massachusetts the great majority of sexual harassment complaints are resolved informally, many of them through the use of mediation.

WHEN IS MEDIATION APPROPRIATE?

1. *Desired by the grievant*

There are many reasons why someone who has been harassed might prefer mediation to a formal hearing or investigation. Among the reasons most frequently mentioned by those who have been harassed are:

a. *faster resolution*—Hearings and investigations take a long time. Most grievants want the matter to be over with as quickly as possible. Mediation can commence soon after the grievant indicates she wants to mediate and it need not go on for a long time.

b. *preserve confidentiality*—Being harassed is often experienced as humiliating. Mediation promises a level of confidentiality that often cannot be matched in a hearing or an investigation.

c. *Avoid the stress of a hearing*—By definition hearings are formal and adversarial. Each party is impelled to present the other in the worst possible light, and to attempt to prove the other wrong. The aim is to win, not to come to an understanding. Often the experience of the hearing is almost as disturbing as the harassment itself. While mediation is not easy, because it is not an adversarial situation, it is not typically as hostile as a hearing.

d. *Focus on education rather than punishment*—For a variety of reasons, many victims of harassment do not want to get the person who harassed them in trouble. At the same time they want the harasser to know what the impact of the harassment has been and they want to keep it from happening again. Often they will pursue a complaint only if they are assured that their complaint will not directly lead to punishment. Mediation can be a means of educating the harasser.

Table 3.4—*Continued*

e. *Restore relations*—In some circumstances the person harassed wishes to reestablish a basis for safely resuming the working relationship with the harasser. Pursuing a formal charge through a hearing would make that unlikely. Mediation can provide a groundwork for rebuilding a working relationship.

2. *Ambiguity of evidence*

There are many instances of harassment that are quite ambiguous. The great majority of sexual harassment cases fall under the hostile environment rubric rather than quid pro quo. Even in some quid pro quo situations, a skilled harasser might be able to mask his intentions and claim miscommunication. Much of harassment is subjective. What one woman finds offensive and disruptive another might find acceptable. In many of the hostile environment situations there is sufficient ambiguity and vagueness that a hearing panel or investigator would be unlikely to conclude that the person charged had in fact violated the sexual harassment policy. Pursuing a formal charge of harassment in these circumstances can be a futile endeavor, only adding to the pain of the person who feels she has been harassed. Mediation can be successful even when there is no clear cut objective evidence of harassment.

HOW IS MEDIATION MODIFIED FOR SEXUAL HARASSMENT CASES?

1. *Individual sessions before joint sessions*

In traditional mediation the parties do not meet individually with the mediator before the first mediation session. At that session both disputants are present and each tells his or her story to the mediator in the presence of the other party. To keep the sessions less volatile and to ensure that the mediation does not become an extension of the harassment, mediators in sexual harassment cases should consider conducting separate sessions with each of the participants to allow for a full venting of the powerful emotions associated with the situation and to assess whether or not mediation has some probability of achieving a solution satisfactory to both parties.

2. *Advisors and support persons*

For the most part mediators prefer to exclude all but the disputants from the mediation sessions. With sexual harassment cases it seems preferable to allow each of the disputants to be accompanied by an advisor. In addition to providing support in an emotionally difficult situation, the advisors can help the disputants realistically assess the options for settlement that emerge during the course of the mediation. In addition, the presence of an advisor often helps balance the disparity of power that exists in many harassment cases. Of course the mediator too, has responsibility to structure the negotiations so as to minimize power imbalances.

Table 3.4—*Continued*

WHAT CAN MEDIATION ACCOMPLISH?

1. *Empowerment of the grievant.*

Mediation is built around the idea of building or restoring trust, equality and mutual respect between the disputants. Sexual harassment represents a violation of trust, equality and respect. Mediation can empower a grievant who feels harassed to approach the harasser as an equal, explaining how trust has been violated, and respect lost. The presence and activity of the mediator can make the grievant feel safe to speak for herself, to the harasser, without having to worry about intimidation.

2. *Develops negotiation skills.*

Mediation creates a forum in which participants clarify their understanding of their own interests, and are supported in negotiating on their own behalf. Disputants learn to take a problem-solving orientation toward their conflicts. The experience in mediation can transfer to other situations that call for skills in negotiation.

3. *Facilitates communication.*

Some sexual harassment cases evolve from differences in life-styles and values. Mediation can provide an arena in which people communicate respectfully about differences, thereby reducing hostilities between them. Especially for people who may have to have some continuing interaction after the mediation, mediation can enhance their ability to communicate with one another.

4. *Mutually satisfactory outcomes.*

Mediation is a method for arriving at solutions that satisfy the needs of all participants to a dispute. Respondents are more likely to be transformed after mediation than after punishment, because they learned through a face to face discussion about the impact of their actions on the person they harassed.

5. *Healing*

If mediation is successful, both the grievant and the relation between the grievant and the respondent can be somewhat healed. Many people who have been harassed report that a successful mediation provided a turning point in moving away from victimhood.

6. *An increase in the number of grievants willing to pursue complaints.*

Many grievants report a reluctance to pursue charges through a formal hearing procedure but a willingness to attempt mediation. At the University of Massachusetts at Amherst only 12 of approximately 125 allegations of sexual harassment (since 1982) have gone to formal hearings. Many of those who chose to pursue their concern through mediation indicated that they would have dropped the charge if they had been required to face a hearing.

Project on the Status and Education of Women
1818 R St NW
Washington, DC 20009

Explanatory Models of Sexual Harassment

Research has indicated that the type of strategy selected in dealing with sexual harassment is related to the explanatory model victims use in explaining their experiences. Three explanatory models of sexual harassment have been proposed (Tangri, Burt, & Johnson, 1982): natural/biological model, organizational model, and sociocultural model. Each model implies several predictions about the likely harassers, the likely victims, the behavior expected, the feelings and responses of victims, the consequences of being harassed, and the work or educational situation conducive to sexual harassment.

The idea that sexual harassment is an inherently personal rather than an institutional matter is a variation on the explanatory framework called the *natural/biological model*. The natural/biological model views sexual harassment is a consequence of natural sexual interactions between people, either attributing a stronger sex drive to men than to women (thus men "need" to engage in aggressive sexual behavior) or describing sexual harassment as part of the "game" between sexual equals. This model obviously can't account for the extreme stress reactions suffered by its victims (and not suffered by their harassers). It is as fallacious as a racist theory that attributes the victimization of minorities to a "natural" prerogative or capacity of a superior race or to the "inevitable" workings of social forces.

The *sociocultural model* posits sexual harassment as only one manifestation of the much larger partriarchal system in which men are the dominant group. Therefore, harassment is an example of men asserting their personal power based on sex. According to this model, sex would be a better predictor of both recipient and initiator status than would organizational position. Thus, women should be much more likely to be victims, especially when they are in male-populated college majors and careers.

This model gives a much more accurate account of harassment since the overwhelming majority of victims are women, and the overwhelming majority of harassers are men (90%–95% in each case; Fitzgerald et al., 1988). Yet it can have the unfortunate effect of leaving women feeling nearly as powerless as the natural/biological model does. If sexual harassment is so ingrained in our whole culture, how can the individual withstand such a massive, systemic force?

The *organizational model* asserts that harassment results from opportunities presented by relations of power and authority, which derive from the hierarchical structure of organizations. Thus, harassment is an issue of organizational power. Since work (and academic) organizations are defined by vertical stratification and asymmetrical relations between supervisors and subordinates, and teachers and students, individuals can use the power of their position to extort sexual gratification from their subordinates.

In our experience, this model is most useful for understanding and opposing harassment in the academy and workplace. But it should be—to obtain the fullest explanatory range and corrective power—combined with the sociocultural model. Organizational power is so pervasively abused, victimizing literally tens of millions of women in the workplace, schools, colleges, and universities, *because* sexual inequality and victimization are endemic to our patriarchal culture.

Currently research has suggested that the explanatory model a woman uses to explain the harassment she has experienced will help to determine the coping strategies she uses. For example, Paludi (1990a) reported that women's adherence to the organizational model promoted their empowerment. Women who employ this explanatory model reported seeking redress within an organization or institution. Such a response would not be predicted from adherence to the sociocultural model: women would not be likely to take interpersonally assertive action or to act on the expectation that the organization will help them resolve the issue. Women are much more likely than men to assign a central role to the college or workplace for preventing and dealing with all levels of harassment. Since the research indicates that men attribute more responsibility to women victims of harassment, men would also be likely to minimize the potential responsibility of college/university officials (Paludi, 1990b).

Summary

In some instances it may be possible to end sexual harassment and gain a sense of security by taking individual action. The most effective response has been to write a letter to the harasser stating what occurred and giving the individual's reaction and her goals for ending or remedying the situation.

In most instances, however, institutional action is necessary to identify, end, and remedy the harassment. Most harassers—as indicated in chapter 1—do not identify their behavior as harassment and persist in it despite clearly negative responses from those they victimize. Academic institutions, businesses, and agencies therefore need to have clear and effective procedures for reporting and investigating charges of harassment. These procedures should include educational material made available to all members of the workplace or academic community. They should also provide informal and nonthreatening contexts to discuss possible incidents of harassment.

Hunter has found that a specially appointed panel is the most effective way to educate the community about sexual harassment and to provide resolutions of both informal and formal complaints. Our Panel, appointed by the president, consists of faculty, staff, and students. Because the Panel is independent of the regular institutional hierarchy and is broadly representative of the college community, individuals have found it easier to contact Panel members.

Those who identify sexual harassment as an abuse of institutional power are more likely to seek remedies from within the structure of the workplace or academic community. Those who see it as a result of "natural" differences between women and men, and those who see its causes only in terms of general cultural sexism, are less likely to take any action to end the harassment.

Although federal and state laws do provide remedies for those victimized by harassment, the means of redress are usually costly, slow, and cumbersome. We strongly recommend that the institution, workplace, or agency take clear and effective corrective action so that further legal action is not necessary. Such legal action always imposes an additional burden on those who already suffered abuse. Federal statutes, in fact, require that procedures for ending sexual harassment and providing corrective action must exist in order for an organization receiving federal funds to be in compliance with Titles VII and IX.

64 *Academic and Workplace Sexual Harassment*

References

Biaggio, M. K., Watts, D., & Brownell, A. (1990). Addressing sexual harassment: Strategies for prevention and change. In M. A. Paludi (Ed.), *Ivory power: Sexual harassment on campus.* Albany: SUNY Press.

Fitzgerald, L. F., Shullman, S., Bailey, N., Gold, Y., Ormerod, M., & Weitzman, L. (1988). The incidence and dimensions of sexual harassment in academia and the workplace. *Journal of Vocational Behavior, 12,* 152–75.

Gutek, B. (1985). *Sex and the workplace.* San Francisco: Jossey Bass.

Licata, B. J., & Treadeau, L. (1986). The frequency, sources, and correlates of sexual harassment among women in traditional male occupations. *Sex Roles, 15,* 433–42.

Littler-Bishop, S., Seidler-Feller, D., & Opaluch, R. (1982). Sexual harassment in the workplace as a function of inititator's status: The case of airline personnel. *The Journal of Social Issues, 38,* 137–48.

Livingston, J. (1982). Responses to sexual harassment on the job: Legal, organization and individual actions. *The Journal of Social Issues, 38,* 5–22.

Loy, P., & Stewart, (1984). The extent and effects of the sexual harassment of working women. *Sociological Focus, 17,* 31–43.

Meek, P. M., & Lynch, A. Q. (1983). Establishing an informal grievance procedure for cases of sexual harassment of students. *Journal of the National Association for Women Deans, Administrators, and Counselors, 46,* 30–33.

Metha, A., & Nigg, J. (1983). Sexual harassment on campus: An institutional response. *Journal of National Association for Women Deans, Administrators, and Counselors, 46,* 9–15.

National Association of College and University Attorneys (1988). *Sexual harassment on campus: A legal compendium.* Washington, D.C.: Author.

Paludi, M. A. (Ed.) (1990). *Ivory Power.* Albany: SUNY. a.

Paludi, M. A. (1990). Creating new taboos in the academy: Faculty responsibility in preventing sexual harassment. *Initiatives, 52,* 29–34. b.

Remick, H., Salisbury, J., Stringer, P., & Ginorio, A. (1990). Investigating complaints of sexual harassment. In M. Paludi (Ed.), *Ivory Power.* Albany: SUNY.

Tangri, S., Burt, M., & Johnson, L. (1982). Sexual harassment at work: Three explanatory models. *Journal of Social Issues, 38,* 33–54.

Terpstra, D. (1986). Organizational costs of sexual harassment. *Journal of Employment Counseling, 23,* 112–19.

Terpstra, D., & Cook, S. (1985). Complainant characteristics and reported behaviors and consequences associated with formal sexual harassment charges. *Personnel Psychology, 38,* 559–74.

Thurston, K. (1980). Sexual harassment: An organizational perspective. *Personnel Administrator, 25,* 59–64.

Truax, A. (1989). Sexual harassment: What we've learned. *Thought and Action, 5,* 25–38.

Underwood, J. (1987). End sexual harassment of employees, or your board could be held liable. *American School Board Journal, 174,* 43–44.

O CHAPTER **4**

*Educating the Campus and
Workplace Communities About
Sexual Harassment*

Overview

How can the workplace and campus be educated about sexual harassment?

A resurgence of racism has troubled college campuses over the past few years and has received considerable public attention. However, the epidemic of sexual harassment in the classroom and in the workplace has received far less attention. In part this may be due to another difference between racist behavior and sexual harassment: the nature of at least the more obvious forms of racism (ethnic slurs and job discrimination) is generally recognized; the nature of sexual harassment is widely misunderstood—by those who harass, and by those who are harassed, and by those who observe or fail to observe harassment. The problem of educating a community about sexual harassment must therefore begin with explanations of the nature of the problem—its legal, organizational, ethical, psychological, and physical dimensions—before any remedy is possible. Our discussions in chapter 1 are designed to provide a basis for an educational campaign.

As we mentioned in chapter 1, the literature on sexual harassment reveals confusion about just what sexual harassment is (Somers, 1982; Betz and Fitzgerald, 1987). Fitzgerald et al. (1988) reported that male faculty members typically do not label their behavior as sexual harassment despite the fact that they readily admit that they frequently initiate personal relationships with women students. Male faculty members denied the inherent power differential between faculty and students, as well as the psychological power conferred by this differential (as salient a force as the power to confer tangible rewards and punishments). This finding supports Pryor's (1987) conclusions that men who are likely to initiate sexually harassing behavior emphasize male social and sexual dominance, and demonstrate insensitivity to other people's perspectives.

Male faculty in the Fitzgerald et al. (1988) study defined situations where faculty-student sexual behavior was permissable: mutual consent, age, or student status (i.e., undergraduate v. graduate student), outcome (i.e., successful v. unsuccessful relationship), and student-initiated relationships. These male faculty offered the following opinions:

> In a classroom setting it is entirely appropriate that personal and professional lives be separated. However, undergraduates doing honor's research and graduate students become junior colleagues; a close personal relationship is to be encouraged.

> Just because I personally haven't engaged in close personal or sexual relationships doesn't mean that I disapprove. Whatever the adults feel that they must do, as responsibly as they can, is just fine.

> It has been my observation that students, and some faculty, have little understanding of the extreme pressure a male professor can feel as the object of sexual interest of attractive women students. (p. 337)

However, because of great differences in power due to organizational and cultural status, there is no such thing as women students' informed consent in a sexual relationship with male faculty members.

Equally troubling, research reported in chapter 1 indicates that the great majority of women who are abused by behavior that fits legal definitions of sexual harassment—and who are traumatized by the experience—do not label what has happened to them "sexual harassment." (Typically, although at least 30% of women college students report being subjected to behavior that constitutes sexual harassment, only 3%–5% call it that.) The general silence about harassment in the community at large—or misunderstanding or ridicule when it is mentioned—serve to deny its victims the ability to recognize what has been done to them. We have seen that this is true even when harassment takes its most violent form; sexual assault or rape. In the University of Massachusetts study only 3% of the 13% of women students who were raped by acquaintances reported the incident; most who did not were unaware that the sexual assault fit the legal definitions of rape.

Because of the absence of a commonly accepted understanding of the nature, extent, and traumatic impact of sexual harassment—and because of the sociocultural forces that condition many women to blame themselves for abuse they have experienced—women who have been victimized often need resources for education and counseling before they can recognize and challenge what has happened to them.

Kenig and Ryan's (1986) research indicates that faculty men were less likely than faculty women to define sexual harassment as including jokes, and unwanted suggestive remarks, looks or gestures. Women faculty were more likely than men to disapprove of romantic relationships between faculty and students. Furthermore, men were also significantly more likely than women to agree with the following statements: "An attractive woman has to expect sexual advances and learn how to handle them"; "It is only natural for a man to make sexual advances to a woman he finds attractive"; and "People who receive annoying sexual attention usually have provoked it." Finally, faculty men were more likely than women to believe that individuals can handle unwanted sexual attention on their own without involving the college or university. Male faculty, thus, view sexual harassment as a *personal*, not as an organizational issue.

Insofar as institutional structures are dominated by traditional masculine perspectives (which can, of course, be fostered by women as well as men) denial of the nature, extent, and seriousness of sexual harassment will continue. Persistent, comprehensive educational strategies are central to any genuine resolution of the harassment that is epidemic in the academic and workplace communities.

Sandler (1988) has offered suggestions for establishing programs to educate the community about this epidemic and to help those who suffer because of it by (1) establishing a policy statement that makes it clear that differential treatment of professional women on campus will not be tolerated; (2) establishing a permanent committee to explore and report on the academic or workplace environment in relation to issues of gender and sexuality; and (3) publishing an annual report on progress in relation to the status of women.

Biaggio, Brownell, and Watts (1990) also offer interventions that can be implemented in order to challenge attitudes that perpetuate harassment: (1) placing items relating to sexist or harassing behavior on teaching evaluation questionnaires; (2) publishing articles on sexual harassment in student newspapers; (3) sharing information about institutional policies that prohibit sexual harassment at new student orientations and dormitories; and (4) establishing community activist strategies to raise public awareness and to protest particular instances of sexual harassment.

The Hunter Panel has implemented several of these interventions. For example, in collaboration with Hunter's Employee Assistance Program, the Panel has facilitated a four-part series on sexual harassment for staff, faculty, and administrators. These workshops include case studies, role playing, and presentations on legal issues involved in sexual harassment. The program objectives include (1) learning how informal and formal power or authority in the university setting is perceived by students and faculty; (2) learning the politics involved in such nonverbal gestures as touch, body position, personal space; and (3) learning the social meanings attributed to behaviors that legally constitute sexual harassment (see table 4.1).

The Hunter Panel also publishes an informational booklet for faculty, *The Student in the Back Row*, which provides several techniques that can be used to help eliminate sexual discrimination in the classroom (i.e., choosing nonsexist course material, not assuming a heterosexist model when referring to human behavior, and monitoring behavior toward men and women in the classroom). (See table 4.2.)

We also present information about sexual harassment to faculty meetings, including departmental and administrative meetings and general sessions of the faculty. In all of these programs we devote considerable time to discussing legal definitions. Case studies that raise legal and ethical issues are presented to stimulate personal reflection and to generate discussion. These case studies illustrate issues in the area of sexual harassment that may not be addressed by policy statements and laws (see table 4.3).

Orientation sessions on sexual harassment should be held for all new employees and students. These sessions should emphasize the nature and extent of harassment; legal definitions and legal responsibilities; the trauma experienced by individuals who are harassed; the damage done to their careers; and the means the institution provides for supporting those who are harassed, for ending harassment, and for punishing harassers when it is appropriate.

Case studies often disclose certain moral conflicts. Research by Paludi et al. (1988) suggests that the moral problem arises from the conflicting responsibilities the woman has (e.g., protecting her

Table 4.1
Sample Workshops for Staff, Faculty, and Administrators

Workshop 1: Sexual and Gender Harassment: Definitions, Incidence, and the Implications for Women's Career Development

Case Studies Dealing with Definitions of Harassment
Discussion of Case Studies
Presentation on Incidence Rates of Sexual and Gender Harassment
Discussion of Incidence Rates
Conclusion
Sharing Initial Reactions to Information Presented
Stereotypes v. Realities

Workshop 2: Sexual and Gender Harassment: Individual, Institutional, and Legal Remedies

Presentation by College Sexual Harassment Panel
Presentation by Legal Counsel
Presentation by Employee Assistance Program
Presentation by National Consultant on Sexual Harassment
Conclusion
Discussion of Remedies of Harassment

Workshop 3: Gender Harassment: Tarnishing the Ivory Tower

Presentation on Gender Harassment
Discussion of Nonsexist Alternatives to Sexist Verbal and Nonverbal
    Communications
Discussion of Perceptual Differences in Verbal and Nonverbal
    Communications
Conclusion
Discussion of Gender Harassment

Workshop 4: Sexual and Gender Harassment: Strategies for Change

Presentation of Power Issues Involved in the Academy
General Discussion of Power, Gender, and Harassment
Conclusion
Discussion of Workshops

grade and future career v. seeking formal redress for the professor's behavior) rather than from competing rights (Tronto, 1987). The responses to the case studies/ethical dilemmas require for their resolution a mode of thinking that is contextual rather than abstract. Women center their responses on their responsibility to relation-

Table 4.2
The Student in the Back Row

Reprinted with permission from Michele Paludi and Richard
Barickman, Hunter College.

The student in the back row may feel sexually harassed even though
the professor has never made any advance or even a direct personal remark.
The student may feel humiliated, embarrassed, or angry . . .

IF the professor regularly tells jokes that present women as sex
objects. . . .

OR habitually uses "he" or "his" to refer to students (even though
75% of Hunter's students are women). . . .

OR listens intently when a male student talks and responds to his
remarks, but only smiles politely when a female student talks. . . .

OR makes derogatory remarks about gays and lesbians . . .

This kind of behavior may seem harmless or trivial to some people; and the
professors who engage in it may have no intent to hurt or embarrass any
student. But according to Title IX of the 1972 Federal Education Amendments, sexual harassment includes "objectionable emphasis on the sexuality
or sexual identity of a student . . . when the intent or effect of the objectionable acts is to create an intimidating, hostile, or offensive academic environment for the members of one sex." The U.S. Department of Education Office
of Civil Rights, the American Council on Education, and the CUNY Board
of Trustees official policy on sexual harassment support this concern with
sexual stereotyping.

Studies of students' reactions to this sort of classroom behavior (such as
the 1980 Report on Sexual Harassment of the National Advisory Council on
Women's Educational Programs); strongly indicate that many students do
feel uncomfortable or abused when sexual discrimination sets the tone of a
classroom. Though it obviously cannot be equated with attempts at seduction or sexual coercion, this sort of discriminatory behavior, called "gender
harassment" is the most widespread form of sexual harassment in the classroom.. According to recent studies, 70% of women college students experience gender harassment during their college years.[1]

The Hunter College Panel on Sexual Harassment has prepared this
pamphlet in order to increase awareness among Hunter faculty of this form
of sexual harassment. It is a step in our effort to promote discussion of the
problem of sexual harassment—and of ways to remedy it—among students,
faculty, and staff at Hunter. The following discussion is adapted from a
pamphlet, *Avoiding Sexual Discrimination in the Classroom*, produced at California State University, Northridge, by the Women's Studies Program Com-

Table 4.2—*Continued*

mitee, with joint sponsorship from the Counseling Center and School of Humanities.

> When the professor lectured, he directed it to the men in the class. They usually sat in a group together, and you could tell where the professor focused his eyes and directed his voice. . . . The professor continually told sexually derogatory jokes about women during class. Most of the women in the class went along with him and laughed at his jokes. I didn't. . . . One time he commented that Ms. M_____ didn't have a sense of humor. I felt a lot of pressure, because I wanted to speak up, but I felt my grade would suffer.[2]

This student is describing her experience with sexual discrimination in the classroom. Discrimination on the basis of gender or sexual orientation, however inadvertent, can discourage students from taking full advantage of their academic experiences. Ideally, the University classroom is a place where information and knowledge are shared equally among students. However, research at a number of institutions—including Barnard, Berkeley, Dartmouth, Harvard, Oberlin, Wisconsin, and Yale—indicates that some male and female instructors behave in ways that demean women or exclude them from full participation in their courses.

Much discriminatory behavior toward students is not deliberate, since most teachers consciously intend to treat all students justly and fairly. Yet faculty have the power to control many events and interactions in the classroom, and in doing so they convey attitudes and values as well as ideas and information. Teachers who make disparaging remarks about, or implicitly devalue women, gays, or lesbians can undermine students' self-confidence and enthusiasm for learning. This negative experience in the classroom can create serious obstacles to students' academic, professional, and personal growth. The impact is similar to the effects of discrimination based on race, religion, age or other physical or cultural characteristics. Thus, a useful test for determining whether behavior is sexist is to imagine addressing similar kinds of behavior to members of a racial minority.

Examples of this kind of sexual stereotyping include the following:

*Explicit use of derogatory terms or stereotypical generalizations, such as "Older women don't belong in college"; "Women have trouble with calculus"; or "Homosexuals engage in self-destructive life styles."

*Use of "humorous" images or statements that demean or trivialize people because of gender or sexual orientation, such as jokes about "dumb blonds," "gay hairdressers," or "lesbian feminists." In many instances women are portrayed primarily as sexual objects, as when slides of *Playboy* centerfolds are used to illustrate lectures in an anatomy class. Women who do not laugh at such jokes may be told (and may believe) that they lack a sense of humor. This accusation ignores the fact that such humor is directed at women.

Table 4.2—*Continued*

*Reinforcing sexist stereotypes through subtle, often unintentional means, such as using classroom examples in which professional people, such as psychologists, managers, or politicians, are always referred to as men (even though many women students plan to enter these fields). Similarly, gays and lesbians may be habitually associated only with certain professions.

*Continual use of generic masculine terms such as "he" or "man" or "mankind" to refer to people of both sexes. Research indicates that these terms evoke masculine images in students' minds and effectively eliminate women as subjects of discourse,[4] even though there may be no intent to do so. References may also be made to men and women as *necessarily heterosexual* ("When you get married and have kids. . . . ").

Examples of discrimination against women as individuals or part of a group may include the following:

*Habitually recognizing and calling on men more often than women in class discussions.

*Interrupting women more often than men, or allowing others in the class to do so.

*Addressing the class as if no women were present by using statements such as "When you were boys. . . . " or "Ask your wives. . . . "

*Listening more attentively and responding more extensively[5] to comments made by men than to those made by women.

*Treating women who ask extensive questions and challenge grades as troublemakers when men are not treated this way. Women returning to college report that some professors seem to feel threatened by their presence since they are more likely to challenge and question than younger women.

THE FACT THAT MUCH SEXUAL DISCRIMINATION is intangible or unconscious permits some well-meaning teachers to dismiss or ignore it. However, there is little doubt that this behavior puts its victims at a distinct educational disadvantage and may have other lasting effects. In particular, such actions can discourage students from participating in class and from seeking help outside of class, can cause them to avoid or drop classes or to change majors, and can undermine their scholarly and career aspirations.

Certainly it would be a mistake to believe that all or most sexual discrimination is intentional. Teachers, like all other people, reflect and transmit unexamined cultural assumptions, which may include the belief that women are less intellectually committed than men and that their work is less competent and important than men's work. These assumptions are not confined to men; women faculty also can discriminate against women in the classroom. And, again, gay men and lesbians may also be the victims of similar stereotypic assumptions. Racial and ethnic biases may also reveal themselves in sexual discrimination.

Even small acts of discrimination are significant because they are part of a pervasive and cumulative pattern of social inequality. Teachers can begin to challenge that pattern first by carefully examining their own feelings

Table 4.2—*Continued*

and preconceptions about the roles of women and men in society, and then by becoming alert to overt and subtle differences in their interactions with men and women in the classroom.

A number of specific techniques are available for helping to eliminate sexual discrimination in the classroom. These include the following:

*When making general statements about women (or any other group), be sure that they are based on accurate information. Universal generalizations about any social group, such as "Women don't think geographically," are likely, at best, to represent uncritical oversimplification of selected norms.

*Avoid "humor" or gratuitous remarks that demean or belittle people because of gender or sexual orientation, just as you would avoid remarks that demean or belittle people because of their race, religion, or physical characteristic. Respect the dignity of all students.

*Avoid using generic masculine terms to refer to people of both sexes. Although the effort to do this may involve some initial discomfort, it will result in more precise communication and understanding.

*When using illustrative examples, avoid stereotypes, such as making all authority figures men and all subordinates women.

*Try to monitor your behavior toward men and women in the classroom. (You might ask a friend to observe your classes.) Ask, for example:

Do you give more time to men than to women students?

Do you treat men more seriously than women students?

Are you systematically more attentive to questions, observations, and responses made by men?

Do you direct more of your own questions, observations, and responses to men than to women?

Do you assume a heterosexual model when referring to human behavior?

*Encourage your department to add a question concerning discrimina tory behavior in the classroom to teaching evaluations.

*Choose course material which does not perpetuate sexual stereotypes.

*Become better informed about sexual discrimination in the classroom. Useful sources on this subject include:

Phyllis Franklin et al., *Sexual and Gender Harrassment in the Academy: A Guide for Faculty, Students, and Administrators* (New York: Commission on the Status of Women in the Professions, The Modern Language Association of America, 1981). Available for $3.50 and $1.00 postage from MLA, 62 Fifth Avenue, New York, NY 10011.

Table 4.2—*Continued*

Guide to Nonsexist Language (Project on the Status and Education of Women, Association of American Colleges, 1818 R St., NW, Washington, DC 20009). Available for $2.00.

Roberta M. Hall and Bernice R. Sandler, *The Classroom Climate: A Chilly One for Women?* (Washington, D.C.: Project on the Status and Education of Women, Association of American Colleges, 1818 R Street, NW, Washington, DC 20009.

Myra P. Sadker and David M. Sadker, *Sex Equity Handbook for Schools* (New York: Longman, Inc., 1982).

The long-term professional rewards of increased understanding and awareness can include better communication with students, improved teaching effectiveness, and eventual realization of equal educational opportunity for all students.

Notes

1. Billie Dziech and Linda Weiner, *The lecherous professor: sexual harassment on campus* (Boston: Beacon Press, 1984).

2. This quote is taken from one of several reports from students in the California State University, Northridge, Women's Studies minor who described their experience with sexual discrimination in the classroom in spring 1983.

3. Roberta M. Hall and Bernice R. Sandler, *The classroom climate: A chilly one for women?* (Washington, D.C.: Project on the Status and Education of Women, Association of American Colleges, 1982), p. 2.

4. See ibid., 1982.

5. Characteristic patterns of speech in women may predispose some teachers to treat them less seriously than men. Men's speech often is more assertive, couched in terms of impersonal abstractions and tough, "devil's advocate" exchanges. Women's speech often is more tentative, hesitant, polite, and deferential. Styles of speech are correlated with gender, and a teacher unconsciously may react more to the style than to the content of a student's utterances. See Hall and Sandler, *Classroom Climate*, pp. 9–10.

6. See Veronica F. Nieva and Barbara A. Gutek, Sex effects on evaluations, *The Academy of Management Review* 5, no. 2 (1980): pp. 267–76.

ships. The moral imperative that emerges repeatedly in research with women who are discussing sexual harassment is an injunction of care (Fuehrer and Schilling, 1988). For male faculty members, the

Table 4.3
Scenarios for Discussing Sexual Harassment

1. Pretend you have just arrived at your first faculty position after completing your Ph.D. Upon your arrival at the department you are met by a full professor in the same department who shows considerable interest in your research and ideas for teaching. You are flattered by his interest and agree to discuss your research over lunch in the faculty dining room. After a few lunches where the conversation is general and social rather than focused on professional issues, you find that he is touching you—rubbing his knees against yours, placing his hand on your back and arms, and once patting you on the bottom. He asks you to meet him off-campus for early dinners. You decline, offering various excuses, and try to maintain a polite but distant tone in your conversations with him. One day he asks you to come into his office to discuss a student who is in a class you teach. Once you are inside the office, he closes the door, moves toward you, and puts his arms around you. You try to push him away but he holds you tighter and tries to kiss you. There is a knock on the door, he releases you, and you open the door and hurry out of the office.

Is this sexual harassment? Why or why not?

If you believe this is sexual harassment, when did the harassment begin?

Does the full professor have a responsibility (moral, legal, professional, or otherwise) to behave differently? Explain.

Do you have a responsibility to behave differently? Explain.

2. At a department meeting, Professor Helmsley, the director of graduate studies, expresses his opinion that undergraduate courses in literature offered under the Women's Studies Program are useless as preparation for

Table 4.3—*Continued*

graduate study. He therefore recommends that they be dropped from the list of acceptable courses for the undergraduate major in literature.

Is this sexual harassment? Why or why not?

If Professor Helmsley expressed a similar opinion during a lecture to his undergraduate class, would he be engaging in a form of sexual harassment?

3. Maria Chin is called into her supervisor's office to discuss her performance evaluation. He shuts the door, puts his hand on her shoulder, and tells her that this evaluation is not at all good, despite her favorable evaluations during her first three months on the job. She begins to cry. He puts his arm around her and hugs her.

Is this sexual harassment? Why or why not?

Does the sex or sexual orientation of the supervisor make any difference in your evaluation of the situation?

4. In her introductory psychology class, Sonia, a Latina woman, notices that her professor smiles and comments on her appearance as a greeting each morning—but that he does not greet any other student in this way. Before his lecture on contemporary sexual roles and behavior, he remarks to the class, "Sonia can probably help us understand this topic since she has to put up with macho types."

Is this sexual harassment? Why or why not?

Table 4.3—*Continued*

If you think harassment has occurred, is all of the professor's behavior harassing?

5. Kevin is taking an introductory English course. His first writing assignment dealt with his uncertainties about being a new student in college, on his own for the first time. When the essays are returned, his has no grade and only the comment, "Please see me." Kevin goes to his teacher's office during the posted office hours. His teacher suggests that they go out for a drink to discuss the essay.

Is this sexual harassment? Why or why not?

Does it matter whether Kevin's teacher is a man or a woman?

A professor, high school teacher, college adjunct, or TA?

6. Maria is taking a course dealing with human physiology this semester. Her professor has been discussing anatomy and today brings in slides to complement his lecture. For twenty-five minutes the class sits through a discussion of male anatomy, complete with slides from Gray's anatomy text book. Following this presentation and class discussion, Maria's professor begins to lecture on female anatomy. He explains that for lack of time he will show only a few select slides that illustrate the points he wants to make about female anatomy. Maria at once notices that the slides are nude photos from men's magazines.

Do you think this illustrates sexual harassment?

Table 4.3—*Continued*

Why or why not?

What should Maria do?

7. Connie is taking a math course that includes a unit on statistics. She knows that this course is important to her career and a good grade in math can increase her chances of getting into graduate school. Connie has been having some difficulty in understanding probability theory. She decides to talk with her professor about this topic. She tells him about her concern about the material and her wish to get a good grade because she wants to go to graduate school. Connie's professor makes it clear that all she has to do is to become sexually involved with him.

Do you think this illustrates sexual harassment?

Why or why not?

What should Connie do?

8. Ruby is taking a laboratory course this semester. She is having a rather difficult time conducting an experiment. She decides to talk with her graduate teaching assistant for the course about her work. While she was discussing the research, her TA suggests that the two of them date. Ruby makes it quite clear that she isn't interested in him romantically. Throughout the remainder of the semester Ruby receives low grades on her research papers. When she asks her TA about his grading system, he replies, "You had your chance."

Do you think this illustrates sexual harassment?

Table 4.3—*Continued*

Why or why not?

What should Ruby do?

moral imperative usually appears as an injunction to protect the power differential (Paludi, 1988).

This research highlights the need to change the relative power of women in the academy, because traditional power differentials support the abuse of power through sexual harassment. Education alone, so long as a hierarchy of abuse persists, will not remedy the problem. Power issues involved in sexual harassment can be discussed in undergraduate and graduate courses. We recommend the use of experiential exercises in discussing harassment (see table 4.4). We also show videos in classes, in monitors located in crosswalks, and in community presentations on sexual harassment (see table 4.5).

We recommend holding conversation hours for residence hall advisors in dormitories and for student orientation programs (see table 4.6). A campus checklist for dealing with sexual harassment is presented in table 4.7.

Finally, we recommend that institutional research be conducted on the status of women and the incidence of sexual harassment. Surveys to be used for this purpose include the Sexual Experiences Questionnaire (see chap. 1) and surveys dealing with perceptions and attitudes about sexual harassment (see table 4.8). Annual reports from this research should be printed in student newspapers and made available for employees, students, and administrators.

Summary

Our experience as coordinators of the Hunter Panel has convinced us that virtually every effort we make to eliminate sexual harassment and to help those who have been victimized by it is part of our educational effort. Often someone who visits us to discuss her

Table 4.4
Experiential Exercises for Class Discussions

1. Ask students to describe the resources available on their campus for dealing with academic and workplace sexual harassment. You may want to invite the individual(s) who deal with sexual harassment complaints to class to discuss the college's policy statement and procedures.

2. Ask students to develop procedures their campus can take for dealing with all levels of harassment, including sexual assault on their campus. Invite students to share this information with various groups on campus, for example, women's center, lesbian and gay students organizations, and the affirmative action office.

3. Ask students to discuss various ways power manifests itself in the classroom, for example, seating arrangements, topics selected, preparation of syllabus, and grading standards. Invite students to design nonhierarchical courses at the college level.

4. Invite students to identify nonsexist alternatives to words and phrases. Some examples: *coed, chairman, manpower, freshman, master's degree*. Distribute copies of guidelines for nonsexist writing. Some useful material include:

> Miller, C., & Swift, K. (1988). *The handbook of nonsexist writing*. New York: Harper.

> Maggio, R. (1987). *The nonsexist word finder: A dictionary of gender-free usage*. Phoenix, Ariz.: Oryx Press.

5. Ask students to design a two-hour workshop on academic sexual harassment, including references to peer harassment, for a first-year student orientation program.

6. Ask students specific questions about their own campus. For example:

> What is the job title of the person(s) responsible for handling complaints of sexual harassment at this institution?

> Does our institution have a Panel on Sexual Harassment to address complaints?

> Is a distinction made between formal and informal complaints?

> Briefly summarize how complaints are handled.

> What is the sex of the individual responsible for handling complaints?

Table 4.4—*Continued*

Does our institution have a peer-counseling system for students who have filed complaints of sexual harassment?

7. Assign students the following book to read: *Professor Romeo* by Anne Bernays. Ask students to rewrite passages of the text using the perspective of (1) the students in the faculty members class, (2) the professor's son, (3) the professor's department chairperson, and (4) the university president.

8. Invite students to list some overtly discriminatory comments they have heard from faculty that they believe have the effect of discouraging (1) women students, (2) lesbian and/or gay students, (3) ethnic minority students, and (4) physically challenged students. Ask students to offer a variety of ways in which discriminatory comments can be handled in class.

9. Ask students to comment on the "silent language" of the classroom. Topics to include: eye contact, nodding and gesturing, posture, and modulating tone. Have students keep a weeklong log of nonverbal behavior on the part of students in your class. Ask students to note gender similarities and differences.

10. Set up a mock courtroom in your classroom. The case on trial: whether gender harassment in the workplace in the form of displaying pictures of nude women taken from "men's magazines" on bulletin boards creates a "hostile environment." Have students prepare arguments for and against.

experience learns for the first time that the emotions and physical symptoms she has experienced are a common result of harassment. She may be speaking to someone who takes her stituation seriously for the first time. Colleagues who joke about harassment may learn something from the seriousness of our responses to what they take to be casual behavior. "Would you joke that way if we were going to a conference on rape or AIDS?" An administrator who has been asking a senior office assistant to bring his coffee is usually surprised to learn how she feels about his requests. The most common forms of harassment are unrecognized by most members of an academic or working community. Any effort that any of us makes to disclose what is still, unfortunately a hidden issue, creates an empowering learning and working atmosphere for us all. Sexual harassment is an issue for all of us who care about our communities.

Table 4.5
Audio-Visual Material

Your right to fight: Stopping sexual harassment on campus
    Affirmative Action AD 301
    University at Albany
    Suny
    Albany, NY 12222

The wrong idea
    Minnesota Women's Center
    5 Eddy Hall
    192 Pillsbury Dr. SE
    University of Minnesota
    Minneapolis, MN 55455

Sexual harassment on campus: Current concerns and considerations
    Center for Instructional Services
    Old Dominion University
    Norfolk, VA 23529

You are the game: Sexual harassment
    Indiana University
    Audio Visual Center
    Bloomington, IN 47405

The power pinch
    MTI Teleprograms
    3710 Commercial Ave.
    Northbrook, IL 60062

Intent vs. impact
    BNA Communications Inc.
    9439 Key West Avenue
    Rockville, MD 20850

Table 4.6
Discussion Sessions with Residence Hall Advisors and
First-Year Students

Outline of Conversation Hour

Introduction

Is this Sexual Harassment? Exercise Dealing with Definitions of Sexual
    Harassment

Discussion of Responses to Exercise

Sexual Harassment: Abuses of Power

Definitions of Sexual Harassment
    Title VII
    Title IX
    College Policy Statement and Procedures
    Equal Employment Opportunity Commission
    Supreme Court

Types of Sexual Harassment
    Gender Harassment
    Seductive Behavior
    Sexual Bribery
    Sexual Coercion
    Sexual Imposition

Incidence of Types of Sexual Harassment on College Campuses

Role of College in Creating an Atmosphere of Trust on Campus

Role of Residence Hall Advisors in Promoting A Harassment-Free
    Community

Distribution of Materials about Sexual Harassment

Open Discussion

Table 4.7
Educating the Campus Community

"Students must get help from their universities in developing moral standards or they are unlikely to get much assistance at all . . . [Schools need to develop] fair rules of conduct that reinforce . . . basic values."
                                        Derek Bok, President, Harvard University

*Include the policy against peer harassment in the Policy Statement on Sexual Harassment.

*Peer harassment policies need to apply to race, disability, and sexual orientation, in addition to sex.

*Include information about academic sexual harassment, including reference to peer harassment, in faculty and student orientation materials.

*Hold a "Peer Harassment Awareness Week" and schedule programs around the issue of lesbian and gay harassment.

*Mention peer harassment in speeches to reinforce its importance as an institutional priority.

*Require that student leaders attend workshops on peer harassment.

*Encourage sororities and fraternities to present programs on peer harassment.

*Include information on sexual harassment, including peer harassment, in packets for transfer students.

*Report annually on sexual harassment, including peer harassment.

*Encourage faculty to incorporate discussions of sexual harassment, including peer harassment, in their courses.

Campus Checklist for Sexual Harassment

Are there policies and effective procedures for dealing with academic sexual harassment? For workplace sexual harassment?

Do the policies forbid peer harassment behaviors, or is it limited to harassment by faculty, administrators, and other staff?

Table 4.7—*Continued*

How do individuals in your campus community learn whom they should see to discuss sexual harassment.

Are there specific individuals to whom individuals can go for help with sexual harassment issues?

Are remedies clear and commensurate with the level of violation?

Does your campus have procedures to inform new faculty, staff, and students about sexual harassment?

Does your campus have a task force or other structure that examines and reports annually on sexual harassment?

Is there a panel or other group that has the responsibility for educating the campus community about sexual harassment?

Are there regular campus workshops on sexual harassment, including peer harassment?

What services are available to individuals who have experienced sexual harassment?

Table 4.8
Surveys on Sexual Harassment

From Michele Paludi and Donald Grimm, Jr.
Hunter College:

On the next few pages you will see a series of interchanges between professors and students and students and students. We would like you to read the passage and then answer a few questions about what you read. There are no right or wrong answers so feel free to give whatever answers you believe describe your opinions.

SCENARIOS DEPICTING VARIOUS LEVELS OF SEXUAL HARASSMENT

1. Describe the professor using the following personality characteristics, using the following scale:

    1. never or almost never true
    2. sometimes but infrequently true
    3. occasionally true
    4. usually true
    5. always or almost always true
       _____ helpful
       _____ cheerful
       _____ moody
       _____ independent
       _____ shy
       _____ conscientious
       _____ affectionate
       _____ assertive
       _____ flattering
       _____ strong personality
       _____ loyal
       _____ unpredictable
       _____ forceful
       _____ feminine
       _____ reliable
       _____ sympathetic
       _____ sensitive to needs of others
       _____ truthful
       _____ understanding
       _____ secretive
       _____ compassionate
       _____ dominant
       _____ masculine
       _____ likable

Table 4.8—*Continued*

_____ warm
_____ tender
_____ friendly
_____ aggressive
_____ inefficient
_____ childlike
_____ competitive
_____ tactful
_____ ambitious
_____ gentle

3. List three reasons why you believe the professor conducted himself in this way.

4. Do you believe the student played a role in what occurred? Explain your answer.

5. Do you believe the student should do and/or say something about what occurred? Why or why not?

6. If you answered Yes to question #5, list three persons/organizations you believe should be notified about what occurred.

7. How do you think the individuals/organizations you listed in item #6 would respond to what the student described?

Table 4.8—*Continued*

8. Would any or all of the following characteristics of the student contribute to your changing your answers to any of the questions in this survey? Explain your answers.

   sex

   race

   age

   year in college

   religion

   sexual orientation

   sexual experience

9. Would any or all of the following characteristics of the professor contribute to your changing your answers to any of the questions in this survey? Explain your answers.

   sex

   race

   age

   rank (e.g., instructor, assistant, associate, or full professor)

   religion

   sexual orientation

   sexual experience

Table 4.8—*Continued*

From Michele Paludi, Hunter College:

Directions: For each of the following statements, indicate whether you agree or disagree, using the following scale:

1. disagree strongly
2. disagree
3. neutral—neither agree nor disagree
4. agree
5. agree strongly

1. A sexually harassed woman is a desirable woman.
2. The extent of the woman's resistance to harassment should be the major factor in determining if harassment has occurred.
3. A sexually harassed woman is usually an innocent victim.
4. Women often claim sexual harassment to protect their reputations.
5. Any woman may be sexually harassed.
6. Many women claim sexual harassment if they have consented to sexual relations but have changed their minds afterward.
7. A woman should not blame herself for sexual harassment.
8. A woman can successfully resist a harasser if she really tries.
9. Sexually experienced women are not really damaged by sexual harassment.
10. Many women invent sexual harassment stories if they learn they are failing a course.
11. It would do some women good to be sexually harassed
12. Women who are good students are as likely to be sexually harassed as women who are bad students.
13. Women do not provoke sexual harassment by their appearance or behavior.
14. Men, not women, are responsible for sexual harassment.
15. Women put themselves in situations in which they are likely to be sexually harassed because they have an unconscious wish to be harassed.
16. In most cases when a woman is sexually harassed, she deserved it.
17. Virtually all women who have reported sexual harassment are able to rebuild their careers and their belief in their own competence.
18. Sexual harassment is not innocent flirtation and women are not flattered by the behavior.

Table 4.8—*Continued*

From Michele Paludi and Pamela Schneider

Instructions: You will see a series of questions dealing with faculty/instructor-student interactions in colleges and universities. We are interested in your perceptions of the frequency of occurrence of a variety of interactions. For each item, please circle the number which most closely describes your best guess of the incidence of each type of interaction described. We are not interested in your actual observations or reports of specific events—just your perceptions. If you circle a 2 or 3, please indicate whether you guess the professors/instructors involved are only women, only men, or involve both women and men by circling F, M, or B, respectively.

Key:
Perceived Frequency:
　　1. Never
　　2. Infrequently or a rarely isolated event
　　3. A fairly regular or common event

Sex(es) of professors involved:
　　F: Female
　　M: Male
　　B: Both female and male

1. A professor/instructor invites undergraduate students to participate in ongoing research projects.
　　1　2　3　　　F　M　B

2. A professor/instructor lends books or journal articles to a student for independent projects.
　　1　2　3　　　F　M　B

3. A professor/instructor asks a student to help re-arrange books in their office.
　　1　2　3　　　F　M　B

4. A professor/instructor raises an exam score after discussing the exam with a student.
　　1　2　3　　　F　M　B

5. A professor/instructor lowers an exam score after discussing the exam with a student.
　　1　2　3　　　F　M　B

6. A professor/instructor tells suggestive stories or offensive jokes to students in class.
　　1　2　3　　　F　M　B

Table 4.8—*Continued*

7. A professor/instructor makes crudely sexual remarks, either publicly in class or to students privately.
   1 2 3   F M B

8. A professor/instructor publishes a paper with an undergraduate student as co-author.
   1 2 3   F M B

9. A professor/instructor assists a student with applications for graduate school admission.
   1 2 3   F M B

10. A professor/instructor makes seductive remarks about women's appearance, bodies, or sexual activities.
    1 2 3   F M B

11. A professor/instructor uses sexist or suggestive teaching materials in classes other than human sexuality.
    1 2 3   F M B

12. A professor/instructor treats students differently because they are male or female.
    1 2 3   F M B

13. A professor/instructor gives students an extension on a term paper.
    1 2 3   F M B

14. A professor/instructor discusses students' personal problems during office hours.
    1 2 3   F M B

15. A professor/instructor suggests that engineering is inappropriate for women or that there must be something wrong with men who want to be nurses.
    1 2 3   F M B

16. A professor/instructor asks a student to babysit for their children.
    1 2 3   F M B

17. A professor/instructor engages in seductive behavior toward a student.
    1 2 3   F M B

18. A professor/instructor has a cup of coffee with a student in the college cafeteria.
    1 2 3   F M B

19. A professor/instructor has a drink with a student in a pub near campus.
    1 2 3   F M B

Table 4.8—*Continued*

20. A professor/instructor gives unwanted sexual attention to a student.
    1 2 3   F M B

21. A professor/instructor attempts to establish a romantic relationship with a student.
    1 2 3   F M B

22. A professor/instructor takes students to professional conferences.
    1 2 3   F M B

23. A professor/instructor propositions a student.
    1 2 3   F M B

24. A professor/instructor offers a student some sort of reward for being sexually cooperative.
    1 2 3   F M B

25. A professor/instructor lends students money.
    1 2 3   F M B

26. A professor/instructor makes unwanted attempts to touch or fondle a student.
    1 2 3   F M B

27. A professor/instructor asks a student to type and do other clerical work in their office.
    1 2 3   F M B

28. A professor/instructor subtly threatens a student with some sort of punishment for not being sexually cooperative.
    1 2 3   F M B

29. A professor/instructor gives a student an incomplete in a college course.
    1 2 3   F M B

30. A professor/instructor makes unwanted attempts to have sexual contact with a student.
    1 2 3   F M B

31. A professor/instructor treats students differently because of their ethnicity.
    1 2 3   F M B

32. A professor/instructor sexually harasses a student.
    1 2 3   F M B

33. A professor/instructor mentors a college student.
    1 2 3   F M B

References

Beauvais, K. (1986). Workshops to combat sexual harassment: A case study of changing attitudes. *Signs, 12*, 130–45.

Betz, N., & Fitzgerald, L. (1987). *The career psychology of women.* New York: Academic Press.

Biaggio, M. K., Watts, D., & Brownell, A. (1990). Addressing sexual harassment: Strategies for prevention for change. In M. A. Paludi (Ed.), *Ivory power: Sexual harassment on campus.* Albany: SUNY Press.

Cyril, J., & Egelman, C. (1988, April). *Educational strategies.* Workshop presented at the Conference on Sexual Harassment on Campus, New York.

Diamond, R., Feller, L., & Russo, N. F. (1981). *Sexual harassment action kit.* Washington, D.C.: Federation of Organization for Professional Women.

Fitzgerald, L., Shullman, S., Bailey, N., Richards, M., Swecker, J., Gold, Y., Ormerod, Mr., & Weitzman, L. (1988). The incidence and dimensions of sexual harassment in academia and the workplace. *Journal of Vocational Behavior, 32*, 152–75.

Fitzgerald, L. F., Gold, Y., Ormerod, M., & Weitzman, L. (1988). Academic harassment: Sex and denial in scholarly garb. *Pyschology of Women Quarterly, 12*, 329–40.

Fuehrer, A., & Schilling, K. M. (1988). Sexual harassment of women graduate students: The impact of institutional factors. *The Community Psychologist, 21*, 13–14.

Hall, R. M., & Sandler, B. R. (1982). *The classroom climate: A chilly one for women?* Washington, D.C.: Project on the Status and Education of Women, Association of American Colleges.

Hite, M. (1988, April). Sexual harassment and the university community. Paper presented at the Conference on Sexual Harassment on Campus, New York.

Jensen, I., & Gutek, B. (1982). Attributions and assignment of responsibility in sexual harassment. *Journal of Social Issues, 38*, 121–36.

Kenig, S., & Ryan, J. (1986). Sex differences in levels of tolerance and attribution of blame for sexual harassment on a university campus. *Sex Roles, 15*, 535–49.

Licata, B. J., & Popovich, P. M. (1987). Preventing sexual harassment: A proactive approach. *Training and Development Journal, 41*, 34–38.

Paludi, M. A. (1988, April). Working 9 to 5: Women, men, sex and power. Paper presented at the New York State Psychological Association, Catskills.

Paludi, M. A, Scott, C., Grossman, M., Matula, S., Kindermann, J., & Dovan, J. (1988, March). *College women's attitudes attributions about sexual harassment.* Symposium presented at the Association for Women in Psychology, Bethesda, Md.

Pryor, J. B. (1987). Sexual harassment proclivities in men. *Sex Roles, 17,* 269–89.

Sandler, B. (1986). *The campus climate revisited: Chilly for women faculty, administators, and graduate students.* Washington, D.C.: Project on the Status and Education of Women, Association of American Colleges.

Sandler, B. (1988, April). Sexual harassment: A New issue for institutions, or these are the times that try men's souls. Paper presented at the Conference on Sexual Harassment on Campus, New York.

Somers, A. (1982). Sexual harassment in academe: Legal issues and definitions. *The Journal of Social Issues, 38,* 23–32.

Stimpson, C. R. (1989). Over-reaching: Sexual harassment and education. *Initiatives, 52,* 1–5.

Tronto, J. C. (1987). Beyond gender differences to a theory of care. *Signs, 12,* 644–63.

Appendix: Sample Articles on
Academic and Workplace Sexual Harassment

Women Students' Assessment of Consensual Relationships with Their Professors: Ivory Power Reconsidered

By: Sue Rosenberg Zalk, Judy Dederich, and Michele Paludi. Reprinted with permission from Sue Rosenberg Zalk.

One of the most persistent problems in the literature on academic sexual harassment concerns the lack of a widely agreed upon definition of the concept (Betz & Fitzgerald, 1987; Crocker, 1983; Fitzgerald, 1990, Paludi, 1990, Somers, 1982). MacKinnon (1979) noted that "it is not surprising . . . that women would not complain of an experience for which there has been no name. Until 1976, lacking a term to express it, sexual harassment was literally unspeakable, which made a generalized, shared and social definition of it inaccessible" (p. 27). Research by Fitzgerald, Shullman, Bailey, Richards, Swecker, Gold, Ormerod, and Weitzman (1988) indicated that undergraduate women typically do not label their experiences as sexual harassment, despite the fact their experiences meet legal definitions and 30%–70% of these women experience one or more types of sexual harassment (i.e., gender harassment, seductive behavior, sexual bribery, sexual coercion, and sexual imposition) each year by one or more of their male professors or graduate teaching assistants.

The subject of this paper is women students who willingly enter into a sexual relationship with a male professor. By "willingly" we mean in the absence of sexual bribery (i.e., the solicitation of sexual activity or other sex-linked behavior by promise of reward) and/or sexual coercion (i.e., coercion of sexual activity or other sex-linked behavior by threat of punishment). We will show how the structure of the academy interacts with psychological dynamics to increase women's vulnerability to seductive behavior (and other types of sexual harassment). We will provide a description of what the relationship looks like through women's eyes. This is a necessary view for establishing campus-wide educational programs concerning sexual harassment (Paludi & Barickman, in press). Behaviors, even emotions, do not exist in a vacuum. As such, an understanding of the woman student engaged in an affair with a professor requires an understanding of the context within which these affairs occur, the academy.

The Academy

The formal academy was instituted to educate men for the betterment of society: Men teaching men. Today, most academic institutions educate women as well as men, but they are still a male domain, dominated by men. Women's very presence in the academy represents their movement out of the private sphere and into male turf and is actively resisted (Paludi & Steuernagel, 1990). Academic institutions are structured hierarchically. The students are at the bottom of the hierarchy, the "officers" are at the top. In the middle sit the professors—with their own hierarchical markers (adjunct, instructor, Assistant Professor, Associate, Full).

College professors are admired. Many people are in awe of professors. They think professors know more than they do and they think professors are smarter than they are. But the professional contributions are generally acknowledged by a narrowly defined group of colleagues. Professors' incomes are limited and their power elusive. Their achievements and status grant them few social "perks."

But there are many benefits to being an academic. In many ways the role of professor in the academy is a unique situation. Tenure, once achieved, means job security. The job is somewhat unstructured and flexible, the range of demonstrable commitment is wide and there is considerable freedom in organizing one's time. In the U.S. professors are given tremendous autonomy. The status of the role and a commitment to academic freedom makes administrators, Deans, chairs and colleagues most reticent to judge a professor's competence or style in carrying out the role (Sandler, 1988). Not surprisingly, there are few guidelines for faculty-student relations. This autonomy exaggerates the professor's sense of self-importance and contributes to arrogance (Dziech & Weiner, 1984). It readily lends itself to feeling "licensed". It also contributes to an aura which shrouds the professor in the eyes of others.

The student, the complement to the professor, enters this setting and must adapt to it—it will not accommodate to her. Although students are at the bottom of the hierarchy (and sadly treated as such), their position is not parallel to those at the bottom of the hierarchy in such institutions as, for example, corporations. Students are not support staff. They do not work for a person or an organization. Theoretically, the organization exists to serve them. The product of their work is theirs. Its assessment is a measure of personal achievement and not of contribution to the organization (Wilson & Krauss, 1983). And students are definitionally non-permanent. They do, and are supposed to, move out and on.

Students attend college to advance themselves intellectually and, as a result, in the social order. The professor is the vehicle for doing this. So the roles of professor and student are intertwined—although it is not an equal partnership. However, the "contract" does not operationalize roles. The scripts are not clearly delineated and the professional role, in relationship to the student, is vague and somewhat confusing. The "job description" outlines professional obligations but hints at roles which nurture the intellectual and emotional maturity of the individual—a task which encourages, perhaps requires, more personal relating (Zalk, in press). The student also struggles with her or his script in the complementary scenario (Fitzgerald, 1986; Fitzgerald & Weitzman, 1990).

Whatever form their relationship takes, students are another source of recognition for the professor. The professor "knows" what the students wants to "know", is looked upon by the student as an authority, as smart, as having "proved" himself/herself in a way students have yet to realize. The professor is often admired, and students frequently believe they will never be as clever, no matter how much they learn.

Power and Faculty-Student Roles

It is not just the distorted aggrandisement by the student or the greater store of knowledge that is granted the professor that frames the student's vision before and during the initial phases of the affair. The bottom line in the relationship is *POWER*. The faculty member has it and the student does not. As intertwined as the faculty-student roles may be, and as much as one must exist for the other to exist, they are not equal collaborators. The student does not negotiate indeed, has nothing to negotiate with. There are no exceptions to this, and students know this.

All the power lies with the faculty members—some of it real, concrete, and some of it is imagined or elusive (Sandler, 1988). The bases of the faculty member's almost absolute power are varied and range from the entirely rational into broad areas of fantasy. Professors give grades, write recommendations for graduate schools, wards and the like, and can predispose colleagues' attitudes towards students. But it goes beyond this. Knowledge and wisdom are power—particularly in the academy the setting within which the student must effectively operate. While superior knowledge, and thus presumably greater wisdom, are often ascribed to faculty members by society at large, the students' adolescent idealism exaggerates its extent. The knowledge and experience ascribed to age add to this source of power. The extension of the power of knowledge is often made into the realm of values and students often accept, uncritically, as true or right what the professor espouses (Stimpson, 1988).

It is easy to see how this imbalance of power exacerbates the vulnerability of all students. One can also understand what a heady experience it is for the student who is singled out as "special" by a professor. There is another dimension to the professor's power which is more elusive. The professor's purpose does not stop at "feeding" information and facts. Professors are expected to mentor by nurturing a student's capacity to think analytically, to reason logically, to harness creativity, in short, to mature intellectually and esthetically. This implies that the professor's power extends over the "minds" of their students. Whether or not this is true, many professors believe it. The most humble refer to it as tapping and nurturing potential; the more grandiose think in terms of unformed minds to be "shaped" (Haring-Hidore & Paludi, 1989). So, the faculty member's aura of power far exceeds his official assessment of students' performance.

Finally, the professor's greatest power lies in the capacity to enhance or diminish students' self-esteem. This power can motivate students to master material or convince them to give up. It is not simply a grade, but the feedback and the tone and content of the interaction. Is the student encouraged or put down? Does the faculty member use his/her knowledge to let students know how "stupid" they are or to challenge their thinking? This is *REAL* power.

Male faculty typically *deny* the inherent power differential between faculty and students, as well as the psychological power conferred by this differential (that is as salient as the power derived from evaluation) (Fitzgerald, Weitzman, Gold, & Ormerod, 1988). Nonetheless, they have chosen this relationship for the unequal balance of power. They feel safer by far holding all the high cards than in relationships of greater equality.

The above blueprint describes the setting in which student/faculty sexual liaisons evolve. It is necessary background for a fuller understanding of the psychology of sexual harassment. Not only is the environment conducive to sexual harassment, but it can stimulate, as opposed to inhibit, emotional needs, conflicts and vulnerabilities, and provides the setting for acting them out (Paludi & Barickman, in press; Reilly, Lott, & Gallogy, 1986). These conflicts are more likely to surface, the terrain nurtures them, and the props are available to perform the script.

What the Woman Student/Lover Sees

What does the woman student, engaged in an affair with a professor, think is going on? The power differential in their respective academic roles is a reality that cannot not be ignored. Does she ask "Why me?" "Why was I chosen by this man who could have smarter, prettier women?" Sure, she does and rarely does she come up with a logical explanation for the emotions she is experiencing. Does she entertain the possibility that she is being exploited? That she may some day view her experience as victimization? According to Koss (1990) and Fitzgerald (1986), rarely!

How, then, does the student who is sexually involved with a professor make sense of the relationship? Some observations (based on clinical treatment and resolving complaints of sexual harassment) of women students during and after these love affairs lends insight.

One of the most striking characteristics of these women is the global undifferentiation of their thinking regarding the affair, although they are capable of sophisticated critical analyses in other areas. This may take the form of a global idealization of the professor which extends to all areas; e.g., "He knows everything!" There is an uncritical insistence that the relationship is truly unique, rarely found in life, outside the application of protocol so rules do not apply. They *truly* understand one another. Their academic roles reflect societal conventions—"spiritually" they are equals and she is his peer. When it is over, one sees a dazed student and hears, "I didn't know what was happening."

Coupled with the lack of critical thinking are passivity and denial. Many women feel compelled to go along with the professor and see no alternatives. Even at the end of the affair, they remain vulnerable to others because they cannot see what they might have done differently. Their passivity is expressed in pervasive learned helplessness; nothing they could do would have any affect on their actions, on the professor, or on the situation as a whole. Denial is an important aspect of this passivity and powerlessness: the student usually not only refuses to recognize that she has choices, but she also does not think that there are risks involved for her. Nor will she even consider the possibility that she is not unique and that the faculty member has a "track record." If confronted with the latter, she dismisses it (Paludi, 1988). "Their" relationship is different.

Students' low self-esteem is a powerful motivation for seduction. They are enchanted by their professor's attentions because they see themselves as terribly inferior, even to their peers, in intellectual capacity and desirability. Thus, they use the relationship either to prove their unworthiness to themselves if they are involved with a professor who treats them poorly, or in a high-risk attempt to disprove their painful self-doubts if the man treats them well.

An adolescent idealization of the professor and all that he "touches" often characterizes these women. At least as long as the affair lasts, the student romanticizes both the man and the affair—thereby also romanticizing herself. They adopt a personal fable (Elkind, 1967) in which they see themselves as someone "special," to whom no harm will come. Again, this idealization proceeds with an abandonment of critical thinking and leaves the student open to devastating hurts from many sources. After the affair, it often leads to bitter shame ("How could I have thought that?") and consequent self-doubt and further lowering of self-esteem.

Even with the reentry, more mature and life-experienced woman, where the pairing might be appropriate outside the academy, within it it generally proves disastrous. These students, relying on having "been around," objectively assess the "match" which seems reasonable on the surface. The are, nonetheless, most unsure of themselves as students (Haring-Hidore & Paludi, 1989). They question whether they can really succeed, measure up, or belong in college at all. Simultaneously, they feel like misfits. They have little in common with other, younger students and are "inferior" to faculty, who may well be their age. The attention of the professor is most affirming and the power differential is ignored in favor of the rationale that he is not only an appropriate match but a good catch.

But the agendas of the pair are different and the revelation that she was "delusional" (rather than mislead) is crushing and intensifies existing doubts.

Even the student who enters such a relationship believing that she can use it for her own ends, thus in fact feeling somewhat powerful, must come under scrutiny. These women are in fact *giving up* control in the *hope* of regaining it later by indirect manipulations of the faculty member. These relationships all too often boomerang, and even when she succeeds in getting what she wanted, she has learned that status can be gained from dependency on powerful men rather than finding out how to use her own independent strengths to make direct achievements.

Whatever their pretense is for getting involved, they are usually setting themselves up for punishment. They have made themselves vulnerable, have proceeded on fantasy assumptions—and feel their worst doubts about themselves have been realized. The exceedingly harsh superegos of these women and the tremendous amount of guilt they experience is striking. Frequently they are overwhelmed with shame, feeling they have revealed the parts of themselves they most despise. Rarely, if ever, will you hear a student simply dismiss the affair, chalking it up to experience.

The View Through A Fog

Although not all students succumb to sexual overtures by professors, some women are more likely to be targeted than others. Sexual harassers appear to favor as their object of attention women who are nonassertive, under a lot of stress, uncertain about their academic endeavors, loners and nontraditional women (Dziech & Weiner, 1984). Dziech and Weiner as well as DeFour (1988) suggested that ethnic minority women and women in male-populated fields are more vulnerable to receiving sexual attention from professors. Ethnic minority women are subject to stereotypes about sex, viewed as mysterious, and less sure of themselves in the academy (DeFour, 1990). Women in male-populated fields are excluded from the men's "fraternity," are in a hostile and threatening environment and in need of a kindly gesture. From the professor's point of view, these women are blurring one of the privileges of being male and threatening one of the roles which provides evidence of his "maleness." In short, although all women students are vulnerable to some degree, male faculty tend to select those who are most vulnerable and needy. As an aside, this choice is not simply to increase the odds of "scoring." The woman's very vulnerability is part of his psychological scenario which reflects and gratifies immature needs and soothes his "open wounds" (Zalk, 1990).

However, it would be a grave error to assume that students who have affairs with professors are "troubled" at the outset, that this may explain their behavior, the distorted thinking and their post-affair reactions. Some of the most "together" students get sexually involved with professors—honor students, students selected as teaching assistants, school leaders—are all ripe for seduction.

Not all students succumb to sexual overtures by professors and it is difficult to isolate a pattern which distinquishes those who do and those who do not. It is complex and a function of a myriad of things—including the match between her emotional constellation and the professor's. But professors sniff this out as best they can. Some even use their position to obtain needed data, e.g., through diaries, journals, and/or invitations for confidences (Paludi & Barickman, in press). But professors, shrouded in their own positional robes, often misread signals and distort interactions (Kenig & Ryan, 1986). They are prone to interpret behaviors within the context of their own needs.

Consequently, being rebuffed can turn ugly—denials and projections frequently follow (Sandler, 1988). All of this needs to be brought back to the structure of the academy. We began this paper with a description of the status hierarchy in the institution and the exaggerated importance granted the professor. We noted the many and complex layers of power which define the student-faculty relationship. What we did not address and want to discuss now, is how this impacts on the student.

Definitions of Sexual Harassment Revisited

While higher educational institutions insist that they are nurturing independence, responsibility and autonomy in their students, there is an ever present authority figure—someone who determines what is required, sets the standards, judges. The individual student is one in a crowd. She can be accepted, dismissed, ignored. She is not important. The student does not have that attitude available to her when evaluating her relationship with the professor. She must please him. She must do as she is told and do it acceptably. Although the young child may have more at stake in pleasing her parents, the power of the professor is in many ways more absolute. The child gets many chances and can demand individual consideration. Not the student. But there is much at stake for the student—the price involves her future as well as her self-esteem. She must adapt to a situation in which she is powerless and accommodate to the almost absolute power others have over her.

A set-up like this triggers passivity, submissiveness, dependency, a need to please. While the educational instruction expands knowledge and trains critical, analytical thinking, the student role encourages a regression. It is the norm for students to experience transferential feelings toward their professors; the design of the academy makes this inevitable. Given all of this, how would you expect a student to process a sexual overture by an admired professor? Would you expect her to say: "I am being victimized"? Would you expect her to view praise, attention, affirmation, an opportunity to align with the source of power with skepticism? To recognize that this highly regarded, admired professor is insincere and exploiting her? Most likely, no.

Crocker (1983) argued that it is important to offer definitions of academic sexual harassment since

> "they can educate the community and promote discussion and conscientious evaluation of behavior and experience. Students learn that certain experiences are officially recognized as wrong and punishable; professors are put on notice about behaviors that constitute sexual harassment; and administrators shape their understanding of the problem in a way that directs their actions on student inquiries and complaints" (p. 697). Thus, a definition of academic sexual harassment sets the climate for the campus' response to incidents of sexual harassment.

Recently, Zacker and Paludi (1989) found that most college campuses have established definitions of academic sexual harassment. These definitions have adapted the Equal Employment Opportunity Commission guidelines on sexual harassment in employment:

> Unwelcome sexual advances, requests for sexual favors, and other verbal or physical conduct of a sexual nature constitute sexual harassment when:
>
> 1. Submission to such conduct is made either explicitly or implicitly a term or condition of an individual's employment or admission to an academic program;

2. Submission to or rejection of such conduct is used as the basis for decisions affecting an individual's employment status or academic standing, or

3. Such conduct has the purpose or effect of substantially interfering with an individual's performance on the job or in the classroom, or creating an intimidating, hostile, or offensive work or study environment.

Women Organized Against Sexual Harassment (1981) at the University of California, Berkeley, proposed four requirements that have been used as a guide by colleges and universities in writing their policy statements concerning sexual harassment: Guidelines must (1) acknowledge sexual harassment as sex discrimination, not as isolated misconduct; (2) refer to a full range of harassment from subtle innuendos to assault; (3) refer to ways in which the context of open and mutual academic exchange is polluted by sexual harassment, and (4) refer to sexual harassment as the imposition of sexual advances by a person in a position of authority. Crocker (1983) pointed out that to be effective, these requirements must (1) recognize the legal basis for university action and place the problem in social context; (2) recognize the need for and value of specific examples that suggest the range of behaviors and experiences considered sexual harassment; (3) recognize the importance of sexual harassment for the integrity of the academy; and (4) recognize that sexual harassment occurs between people who have unequal power.

Defining academic sexual harassment from organizational and sociocultural power perspectives has been interpreted by some colleges and universities as including consensual relationships. Zacker and Paludi (1989) reported that some campuses have adopted a policy statement that includes information about consensual relationships. For example, the University of Iowa's policy on sexual harassment includes the following statement:

Amorous relationships between faculty members and students occurring outside the instructional context may lead to difficulties. Particularly when the faculty member and student are in the same academic unit or in units that are academically allied, relationships that the parties view as consensual may appear to others to be exploitative. Further, in such situations (and others that cannot be anticipated), the faculty member may face serious conflicts of interest and should be careful to distance himself or herself from any decisions that may reward or penalize the student involved. A faculty member who fails to withdraw from participation in activities or decisions that may reward or penalize a student with whom the faculty member has or has had an amorous relationship will be deemed to have violated his or her ethical obligation to the student, to other students, to colleagues, and to the University.

Harvard University's policy on sexual harassment also includes a statement about consensual relationships:

> Amorous relationships that might be appropriate in other circumstances are always wrong when they occur between any teacher or officer of the University and any student for whom he or she has a professional responsibility. Further, such relationships may have the effect of undermining the atmosphere of trust on which the educational process depends. Implicit in the idea of professionalism is the recognition by those in positions of authority that in their relationship with students there is always an element of power. It is incumbent upon those with authority not to abuse, nor to seem to abuse, the power with which they are entrusted. . . . Even when both parties have consented to the development of such a relationship, it is the officer or instructor who, by virtue of his or her special responsibility, will be held accountable for unprofessional behavior. Because graduate student teaching fellows, tutors, and undergradutate assistants may be less accustomed than Faculty members to thinking of themselves as holding professional responsibilities, they would be wise to exercise special care in their relationships with students whom they instruct or evaluate. . . . Relationships between officers and students are always fundamentally asymmetric in nature.

Including consensual relationships as part of the definition of academic sexual harassment has been met with great resistance (Sandler, 1988; Zacker & Paludi, 1989). Faculty men are less likely than faculty women to include consensual relationships in their definition of sexual harassment (Fitzgerald et al., 1988; Kenig & Ryan, 1986). Faculty men are also less likely than faculty women to define academic sexual harassment to include jokes, teasing remarks of a sexual nature and unwanted suggestive looks or gestures. Men are also significantly more likely than women to agree with the following statements: "An attractive woman has to expect sexual advances and learn how to handle them," "It is only natural for a man to make sexual advances to a woman he finds attractive," and "People who receive annoying sexual attention usually have provoked it" (Kenig & Ryan, 1986). Finally, faculty men are more likely than women to believe individuals can handle unwanted sexual attention on their own without involving the college or university. Male faculty, thus, view sexual harassment as a *personal*, not an organizational issue.

Since research indicates that men attribute more responsibility to women victims of sexual harassment, men would also be likely to minimize the potential responsibility of college/university officials. Within the academic community, faculty and students, and women and men within these groups, have differing resources that are important influences on their investment in academic sexual harassment (Hite, 1990; Kenig & Ryan, 1986). Jensen and Gutek (1982) concluded that "it is reasonable to suggest that male respondents, not wanting to be blamed in the future, would assign more responsibility to the women, and similarly, the women, not wanting to be blamed should such an event happen to them in the future, would assign less responsibility to the women and more to the men" (p. 125). Since the research indicates that victims of sexual harassment are mostly women (see Fitzgerald, Shullman, Bailey, Richards, Swecker, Gold, Ormerod, & Weitzman, 1988 for a discussion of this issue) this means that men would tend to shift responsibility to women victims more than would women (Kenig & Ryan, 1986; Paludi, 1988). The data thus suggests that education is needed in men's perceptions of the misuse of power, their perceptions about women who have been harassed, and their attitudes toward sexual interactions (Paludi & Barickman, in press).

Cyril and Egelman (1988) offered suggestions for addressing sexual harassment on campus, including: (1) conducting information sessions for faculty, staff, and students on the policy toward sexual harassment on campus; (2) holding noontime brown bag seminars on the issue; (3) using peer educators among students; and (4) including materials on sexual harassment in courses on human sexuality. Biaggio, Brownell, and Watts (1990) also offered interventions that can be implemented in order to challenge attitudes that perpetuate harassment: (1) placing items relating to sexist comments or sexual invitations on teaching evaluations, (2) publishing articles on sexual harassment in student newspapers; (3) disseminating information about institutional policies that prohibit sexual harassment at new student orientations and dormitories, and (4) setting up community activist strategies to raise public awareness and to protest particular instances of sexual harassment.

The Hunter College Sexual Harassment Panel (Paludi & Barickman, in press) has implemented several of these interventions. For example, in collaboration with Hunter's Employee Assistance Program, the Sexual Harassment Panel facilitates a four-part series on sexual harassment for faculty and administrators. These workshops include case studies, role playing, and presentations on legal issues involved in sexual harassment. The program objectives include (1) learning how informal and formal power or authority in the university setting is perceived by students and faculty, (2) learning the politics involved in such nonverbal gestures as touch, body position, personal space, and (3) learning the social meanings attributed to behaviors that legally constitute sexual harassment.

In all of these strategies, a considerable amount of time is devoted to the labeling of legally defined behaviors as sexual harassment. Case studies are presented to generate personal examination and generate discussion. These dilemmas point out a continuum of issues in the area of academic sexual harassment which are not addressed by policy statements and laws. As Sandler (1988) argued, faculty responsibility is the only way to ensure a campus free of sexual harassment.

The academy needs what Mead (1978) argued was necessary for the workplace: "new taboos" not new laws against sexual harassment. Creating new taboos in the academy demands that faculty make new norms, not rely on masculine biased definitions of success, career development, sexuality, and power. Creating new taboos calls for a new ethic that will refuse to blame the victim and that will foster an environment that will be compatible with the needs of women students, providing them with equal opportunities to acquire an education in a climate free of sexual and gender harassment. What this new ethic requires, as Stimpson (1988) argued, is to work on what the academy would look like that took *caring* as a central value and how the academy could be structured to faciltate this caring.

The description provided previously of how women students view their affairs in the initial stages tempts the assumption that the woman who has an affair with a professor is an atypical prototype, prone to misjudgement, operating in a somewhat colored reality. This is definitely *not* the case. These descriptions may represent a lapse in objectivity but they are not bizarre. They are defensive strategies, albeit counterproductive, for coping with a situation in which the "facts", as they are known, appear not true and the rules that were taught no longer apply. All women are vulnerable in such situations.

References

Betz, N., & Fitzgerald, L. F. (1987). *The career psychology of women.* New York: Academic Press.

Biaggio, M. K., Brownell, A., Watts, D. (in press). Addressing sexual harassment: Strategies for prevention and change. In M. A. Paludi (Ed.), *Ivory power: Sexual and gender harassment in the academy.* Albany: State University of New York Press.

Crocker, P. (1983). An analysis of university definitions of sexual harassment. *Signs, 8,* 696–707.

Cyril, J., & Egelman, C. (1988, April). *Educational strategies.* Workshop presented at the Conference on Sexual Harassment on Campus, New York, NY.

DeFour, D. C. (1988, July). *Racism and sexism in the academy.* Paper presented at the International Congress on Victimology, Tuscany, IT.

DeFour, D. C. (in press). The interface of racism and sexism in the academy. In M. A. Paludi (Ed.), *Ivory power: Sexual and gender harassment in the academy.* Albany: State University of New York Press.

Dziech, B., & Weiner, L. (1984). *The lecherous professor.* Boston: Beacon Press.

Fitzgerald, L. F. (1986, August). *The lecherous professor: A study in power relations.* Paper presented at the American Psychological Association, Washington, D.C.

Fitzgerald, L. F. (1990). Sexual harassment: The definition and measurement of a construct. In M. A. Paludi (Ed.), *Ivory power: Sexual harassment on campus.* Albany, NY: SUNY Press.

Fitzgerald, L., Shullman, S., Bailey N., Richards, M., Swecker, J., Gold, Y., Ormerod, M., & Weitzman, L. (1988). The incidence and dimensions of sexual harassment in academia and the workplace. *Journal of Vocational Behavior, 32,* 152–175.

Fitzgerald, L. F., Gold, Y., Ormerod, M., & Weitzman, L. (1988). Academic harassment: Sex and denial in scholarly garb. *Psychology of Women Quarterly, 12,* 329–340.

Fitzgerald, L. F., & Weitzman, L. (1990). Men who harass; Speculation and data. In M. A. Paludi (Ed.) *Ivory power: Sexual harassment on campus.* Albany, NY: SUNY Press.

Fuehrer, A., & Schilling, K. M. (1988). Sexual harassment of women graduate students: The impact of institutional factors. *The Community Psychologist, 21,* 13–14.

Haring-Hidore, M., & Paludi, M. (1989). Sexuality and sex in mentoring and tutoring: Implications of opportunities and achievement. *Peabody Journal of Education, 64,* 164–172.

Hite, M. (1990). Sexual harassment and the university community. *Initiatives, 52,* 11–15.

Jensen, I. W., & Gutek, B. (1982). Attributions and assigment of responsibility in sexual harassment. *Journal of Social Issues, 38,* 121–136.

Kenig, S., & Ryan, J. (1986). Sex differences in levels of tolerance and attribution of blame for sexual harasment on a university campus. *Sex Roles, 15,* 535–549.

Koss, M. P. (1990). Changed lives: The psychological impact of sexual harassment. In M. A. Paludi (Ed.) *Ivory power: Sexual harassment on campus.* Albany, NY: SUNY Press.

MacKinnon, C. (1979). Sexual harassment of working women. New Haven: Yale University Press.

Mead, M. (1978). A proposal: We need taboos on sex at work. Reported in B. Dzeich & L. Weiner (1984). *The lecherous professor.* Boston: Beacon Press. Paludi, M. A. (1988, April). Working 9 to 5: Women, men, sex and power. Paper presented at the New York State Psychological Association, Catskills, NY.

Paludi, M. A. (Ed.) (1990). *Ivory power: Sexual harassment on campus.* Albany, NY: SUNY Press.

Paludi, M. A., & Barickman, R. B. (in press). Sexual harassment of students: Victims of the college experience. In E. Viano (Ed.), *Victimization: An international perspective.* New York: Springer.

Paludi, M. A., & Steuernagel, G. A. (Eds.) (1990). *Foundations for a feminist restructuring of the academic disciplines.* New York: Haworth Press.

Reilly, M., Lott, B., & Gallogy, S. (1986). Sexual harassment of university students. *Sex Roles, 15,* 333–358.

Sandler, B. (1988, April). Sexual harassment: A new issue for institutions, or these are the times that try men's souls. Paper presented at the Conference on Sexual Harassment on Campus, New York, NY.

Somers, A. (1982). Sexual harassment in academe: Legal issues and definitions. *The Journal of Social Issues, 38,* 23–32.

Stimpson, C. (1988, April). Overreaching: Sexual harassment and education. Paper presented at the Conference on Sexual Harassment on Campus, New York, NY.

Wilson, K., & Krauss, L. (1983). Sexual harassment in the university. *Journal of College Student Personnel, 24,* 219–224.

Zacker, M., & Paludi, M. A. (1989). Educational programs for academic sexual harassment. Unpublished manuscript, Hunter College.

Zalk, S. R. (in press). Men in the academy: A psychological profile of harassment. In M. A. Paludi (Ed.) *Ivory power: Sexual harassment on campus.* Albany, NY: SUNY Press.

O   APPENDIX **2**

Overreaching: Sexual Harassment and Education

By: Catharine R. Stimpson. Reprinted with permission from Initiatives

Sexual harassment is an ancient shame that has become a modern embarrassment. Largely because of the pressure of feminism
and feminists, such a shift in status took place during the 1970s.
Today, the psychological and social pollution that harassment spews
out is like air pollution. No one defends either of them. We have
classified them as malaises that damage people and their environments. For this reason, both forms of pollution are largely illegal. In
1986, in *Meritor Savings Bank v. Vinson,* the Supreme Court held an
employer liable for acts of sexual harassment that its supervisory
personnel might commit.

Yet, like air pollution, the psychological and social pollution of
sexual harassment persists. In stratosphere, chlorofluorocarbons
from aerosol sprays and other products break apart and help to de-
stroy the ozone layer. Well below the stratosphere, in classrooms
and laboratories, sexual louts refuse to disappear, imposing themselves on a significant proportion of our students[1] As the graduate
dean at a big public university, I experience, in my everyday life, the
contradiction between our disapproval of sexual harassment and the
raw reality of its existence. I work, with men and women of good
will, to end harassment. We must work, however, because the harassers are among us.

Inevitably, then, we must ask why sexual harassment persists,
why we have been unable to extirpate this careless and cruel habit
of the heartless. As we know, but must continue to repeat, a major
reason is the historical strength of the connections among sexuality,
gender, and power. But one demonstration of the force of these
connections, sexual harassment, floats at the mid-point of an ugly,

115

long-lasting continuum. At the most glamorous end of the continuum is a particular vision of romance, love, and erotic desire. Here
men pursue women for the mutual pleasure. That promise of pleasure masks the inequities of power. "Had we but world enough,
and time," a poet sings, "This coyness, Lady, were no crime." But
for the poet, there is not enough world, not enough time. The lady,
then, must submit to him before . . . "Worms shall try / That long
preserv'd Virginity." At the other end of the continuum is men's
coercion of women's bodies, the brutalities of incest and of rape, in
which any pleasure is perverse.

In the mid-nineteenth century, Robert Browning wrote a famous
dramatic monologue, "Andrea Del Sarto." In the poem, a painter is
using his wife as a model. As he paints, he speaks, muses, and
broods. He is worried about his marriage, for his model/wife is apparently faithless, a less than model wife. He is worried about his
art, for his talents may be inadequate. He is, finally, worried about
his reputation, for other painters may be gaining on and surpassing
him. In the midst of expressing his fears, he declares, "Ah, but a
man's reach should exceed his grasp / Or what's a heaven for. . . . "
Traditional interpretations of this poem have praised Browning for
praising the necessity of man's ambitions, of man's reaching out for
grandeur. Indeed, Del Sarto, in an act of minor blasphemy, casts
heaven not as God's space but as man's reminder that he has not yet
achieved his personal best. Unhappily, these interpretations go on,
women can hurt men in their noble quests. Fickle, feckless, the fem-
inine often embarks on her own quest, a search-and-destroy mission
against male grandeur.

A revisionary interpretation of "Andrea Del Sarto," however,
can find the poem a different kind of parable about sexuality, gender, and power. In this reading, a man has at least two capacities.
First, he can reach out and move about in public space and historical
time. Del Sarto goes after both canvas and fame. Next, he can define
a woman's identity, here through talking about her and painting her
portrait. Del Sarto literally shapes the image of his wife. Ironically,
he wants to believe that he is a victim. He exercises his powers in
order to demonstrate that he is powerless. A man, he projects himself as a poor baby who cannot shape up his mate.

A sexual harasser in higher education reveals similar, but more
sinister, capacities. The hierarchical structure of institutions sends
him a supportive message: the arduous climb up the ladder is worth
it. The higher a man goes, the more he deserves and ought to enjoy
the sweetness and freedoms of his place.[2] First, a man reaches out

for what he wants. He makes sexual "advances." His offensive weapons can be linguistic (a joke, for example) or physical (a touch). He warns the powerless that he has the ability to reach out in order to grasp and get what he wants. He also demonstrates to himself that he is able to dominate a situation. As the psychoanalyst Ethel Spector Person has pointed out, for many men, sexuality and domination are inseparable. To be sexual is to dominate and to be reassured of the possession of the power to dominate, (Person, 1980).[3]

Usually, women compose the powerless group, but it may contain younger men as well, the disadvantages of age erasing the advantages of gender. One example: a 1986 survey at the University of Illinois/Champaign-Urbana found that 19 percent of the female graduate students, 10 percent of the undergraduates, and 8 percent of the professional school students had experienced harassment. So, too, had 5 percent of the male respondents. In all but one incident, the harasser was another man (Allen & Okawa, 1987.)

Second, the harasser assumes the right to define the identity of the person whom he assaults. To him, she is not mind, but body; not student, not professional, but sexual being. She is who and what the harasser says she is. Ironically, like Andrea Del Sarto, many academics project their own power onto a woman and then assert that she, not he, has power.[4] He, not she, is powerless. Her sexuality seduces and betrays him. This psychological maneuver must help to explain one fear that people express about sexual harassment policies—that such policies will permit, even encourage, false complaints against blameless faculty and staff. A recent study found 78 percent of respondents worried about loss of due process and about the fate of innocent people who might be accused of misconduct. Yet, the study concluded, less than 1 percent of all sexual harassment complaints each year *are* false. The deep problem is not wrongful accusations against the innocent, but the refusal of the wronged to file any complaint at all. In part, they believe they should handle sexual matters themselves. In part, they hope the problem will go away if they ignore it. In part, they fear retaliation, punishment for stepping out of line. (Robertson, Dyer, & Campbell, 1988).

The unreasonable fear about false complaints is also a symptom of the blindness of the powerful to the realities of their own situation. They enjoy its benefits but are unable to see its nature and costs to other people. They are like a driver of an inherited sports car who loves to drive but refuses to learn where gas and oil come from, who services the car when it is in the garage, or why pedestrians might shout when he speeds through a red light. In a probing essay, Molly Hite (1988) tells a story about a harasser on a United States campus, a powerful professor who abused his authority over female graduate students. He damaged several women, psychologically and professionally. Yet, even after that damage became public knowledge, he survived, reputation intact, although he did discreetly move to another campus. Hite inventories the responses of her colleagues to this event. Men, no matter what their academic rank, tended to underplay the seriousness of his behavior. They thought that he had acted "normally," if sometimes insensitively, that the women had acted abnormally and weakly. Women, no matter what their academic rank, tended to sympathize with the female victims. They could identify with powerlessness. Hite writes,

> "The more the victim is someone who could be you, the easier it is to be scared. By the same reasoning, it's possible to be cosmically un-scared, even to find the whole situation trivial to the point of absurdity, if you can't imagine ever being the victim" (p. 9).

So far, higher education has participated in building at least four related modes of resistance to sexual harassment. First, we have named the problem *as a problem*. We have pushed it into public consciousness as an issue. The Equal Employment Opportunity Commission guidelines, in particular, have provided a citable, national language with which to describe harassment, a justifiable entry in the dictionary of our concerns. Next, we have learned how much administrative leadership has mattered in urging an institution to address this concern. Not surprisingly, faculties have not moved to reform themselves. Next, workshops that educate people about the nature of harassment do seem to reduce its virulence. Finally, we have created grievance procedures with which we can hear complaints, investigate them, and punish harassers.[5] The most carefully designed in themselves help to empower women. The process does not itself perpetuate her sense of self as victim (Hoffman, 1986).

These modes of resistance, good in themselves, have also done good. They have shown an institution's commitment to a fair, non-polluting social environment. They have warned potential harassers to stop. They have offered some redress to the harassed. Resistance will, however, be of only limited good unless a rewriting of the historical connections among sexuality, gender, and power accompanies it. Similarly, putting up traffic lights on crowded streets is good. Lights are, however of only limited good unless drivers be-

lieve in the rights of other drivers, in safety, and in the limits of
their machines.

In such a rewriting, an act of "over-reaching" will be interpreted not as aspiration and desire, but as an invasion of another
person's body, dignity, and livelihood. No one will feel the ap-
proaching grasp of the harasser as a welcome clasp. Over-reaching
will be a sign not of grace but of disgrace, not of strength but of
callousness and, possibly, anxiety, not of virility but of moral and
psychological weakness. It will not be a warm joke between erotic
equals, but a smutty titter from an erotic jerk. The rhetoric of neither
romance nor comedy will be able to paint over the grammar of
exploitation.[6]

One consequence of this rewriting will be to expand our modes
of resistance to include a general education curriculum, not simply
about harassment as a phenomenon, but about power itself, which
harassment symptomizes. This will mean teaching many men to cut
the ties among selfhood, masculinity, and domination. It will mean
teaching many women to cut the ties among self, femininity, and
intimacy at any price, including the price of submission. Occasion-
ally, reading a sexual harassment complaint from a young woman, I
have asked myself, in some rue and pain, why she has acted *like a
woman*. By that, I have meant that her training for womanhood has
taught her to value closeness, feeling, relationships. Fine and dandy,
but too often, she takes this lesson to heart above all others.

The first part of the curriculum, for women, will remind them
of their capacity for resistance, for saying no. Telling a harasser to
stop can be effective.[7] Speaking out, acting verbally, can also empower an individual woman. Less fortunately, these speech acts re-
constitute the traditional sexual roles of man as hunter, woman as
prey. Unlike a rabbit or doe, she is responsible for setting the limits
of the hunt, for fencing in the game park. If the hunter violates
these limits, it is because she did not uphold them firmly enough.
Moreover, saying no to the aggressor also occurs in private space.
Because of this location, both harasser and harassed can forget that
these apparently private actions embody, in little, grosser structures
of authority.

The second part of the curriculum will be for men and women.
Fortunately, women's studies programs are now developed enough
to serve as a resource for an entire institution that chooses to offer
lessons about gender and power. These lessons will do more than
anatomize abuses. They will also present an ethical perspective,
which the practices of colleges and universities might well represent.

This ethic will cherish a divorce between sexuality and the control of another person, an unbridgeable distance between a lover's pleasure and a bully's threat. This ethic will also ask us to cherish our capacities to care for each other, to attend to each other's needs without manipulating them.[8] We will reach out to each other without grasping, hauling, pushing, mauling.

The struggle against sexual harassment, then, is part of a larger struggle to replant the moral grounds of education. Our visionary hope is that we will, in clean air, harvest new gestures, laws, customs, and practices. We will still take poets as our prophets. When we do so, however, we might replace the dramatic monologue of a fraught, Renaissance painter with that of a strong-willed, late twentieth-century feminist. In 1977, in "Natural Resources," Adrienne Rich spoke for those who stubbornly continue to believe in visionary hope.

> "My heart is moved by all I cannot save:
> so much has been destroyed.
> I have to cast my lot with those
> who age after age, perversely,
> with no extraordinary power,
> reconstitute the world."

Notes

1. The authors of a survey of 311 institutions of higher education, conducted in 1984, estimate that one woman out of four experiences some form of harassment as a student. (Robertson et al., 1988). A survey of a single institution, a large public research university, found that 31 percent of the more than 700 respondents had been subjected to "sex-stereotyped jokes, remarks, references, or examples" ("Survey documents," 1988, pp. 41–42).

2. As Robertson et al. comment," individuals in positions of authority . . . (are) used to viewing professional status as expanding privilege rather than increasing responsibility and obligation" (p. 808). An anecdote illustrates this generalization. Recently, I was chairing a meeting of the graduate faculty of my university. Our agenda item was a proposal to conduct a periodic review of faculty members, program by program, to help insure they were still qualified to be graduate teachers. A professor, well-known for his decency, stood up in opposition. He said, "When I got tenure, I became a member of a club, and no one is going to tell me what to do. If I don't want to publish, that's my business."

3. Not coincidentally, most of the sexual harassers whom I have had to investigate as graduate dean have had streaks of arrogance, flare-ups of vanity. In contrast, the men who have been most sympathetic to the necessity of my investigations have had a certain ethical poise, a balance of standards and stability.

4. An obvious parallel is a traditional response to rape, in which women are held culpable for being raped. Moreover, like versions of Jezebel, they are thought only too likely to cry rape in order to cover up their own sins.

5. I am grateful to Robertson et al. (1988) for their description of various modes of resistance to harassment. Their study also explores the reasons why public institutions have been more sensitive than private institutions. More specifically, Beauvais (1986) describes workshops that deal with harassment for residence hall staff at the University of Michigan.

6. Disguising the language of harassment as humor has several advantages. First, it draws on our old, shrewd assessment of much sexual behavior as funny and comic. Next, it simultaneously inflates the harasser to the status of good fellow, able to tell a joke, and deflates the harassed to the status of prude, unable to take one.

7. Allen and Okawa (1987) say that this worked for two-thirds of the respondents in their study of harassment at the University of Illinois.

8. Tronto (1987) suggestively outlines a theory of care that educational institutions might adopt.

References

Allen, D., & Okawa, J. B. (1987). A counseling center looks at sexual harassment. *Journal of the National Association for Women Deans, Administrators, and Counselors, 51*(1), 9–16.

Beauvais, K. (1986). Workshops to combat sexual harassment: A case study of changing attitudes. *Signs, 12*(1), 130–145.

Hite, M. (1988). Sexual harassment and the university community. Unpublished manuscript.

Hoffman, F. L. (1986). Sexual harassment in academia. *Harvard Educational Review, 56*(2), 105–121.

Person, E. (1980). Sexuality as the mainstay of identity. In C. R. Stimpson, & E. S. Person (eds.), *Women: Sex and sexuality.* Chicago: University of Chicago Press.

122   *Academic and Workplace Sexual Harassment*

Robertson, C., Dyer, C. C., & Campbell, D'A. (1988). Campus harassment: Sexual harassment policies and procedures at institutions of higher learning. *Signs*, 13(4), 792–812.

Survey documents sexual harassment at U Mass. (1988). *Liberal Education*. 74(2), 41–2.

Tronto, J. C. (1987). Beyond gender differences to a theory of care. *Signs*, 12(4), 644–663.

The Organizational Context of Sexual Harassment

Presented at the American Psychological Association Convention, August 1989. Reprinted with permission from Karen Maitland Schilling and Ann Fuehrer, Miami University.

Adopting an individual level of analysis to understand sexual harassment, whether one focused on victim blame or psychopathology of the harasser, appears to ignore the prevalence data which would suggest that we would observe anywhere from 30% to 60% of the adult population to be acting out serious psychopathology in their day-to-day work environments. In addition, a number of feminist scholars conceptualize sexual harassment as a pattern of interpersonal behavior that functions at the social structural level to reinforce and perpetuate the subordination of women as a class. Hoffman (1986) argues that "in this view sexual harassment is a manifestation of the differences in power between the sexes and is a form of discrimination through which inequality at the institutional level is maintained." Meg Bond's findings that women who are *aware* of sexual harassment in a university environment reported as adverse consequences of harassment as many of those directly affected would also suggest the wisdom of adopting a more systemic perspective.

Russell (1984) goes beyond an individual level of analysis to identify a number of factors which enhance the likelihood that sexual harassment of women will be found acceptable. According to Russell, harassment may be seen as a form of social control by which women are kept in their rightful subordinate roles. This limiting of women's status in the workplace or learning environment is seen as a natural response on the part of men to women's attempts to gain more power by leaving their appropriate places in the home, in order to achieve equality. By sexualizing interactions with women in the workplace or university setting, men call attention to women's sexuality and passivity, thereby detracting from women' work. Ultimately, women's ambitions are curtailed (Goodman, 1978).

Although the context within which sexual harassment occurs, according to Russell, is one of societal norms which support the sexual subordination of women, in this view the agent of discrimination is the individual male who is interested in demonstrating his ability to dominate individual women. Such an attribution of individual agency is similar to Dziech and Weiner's (1984) identification of harassment as individual pathology. In their book, *The Lecherous Professor: Sexual harassment on campus,* Dziech and Weiner acknowledge that institutional responses perpetuate the occurrence of sexual harassment. However, in examining the etiology of harassment they emphasize factors in individual developmental histories that predispose one to be a harasser. They suggest that harassers are men who experience unresolved adolescent conflicts, who suffered severe ego injuries in high school because they were not members of the most popular group of athletes. In order to acquire a potent masculine self-image, these men engage in behaviors which conform to "a crude extension of the norms some consider acceptable for males" (p. 126). That is, they look to the formation of relationships with female students as a way of establishing masculine identity.

Rather than changing the level of analysis from the systemic to the individual, as Dziech and Weiner do, it seems important to pursue an institutional level of analysis to explain the prevalence of sexual harassment, and to recognize more explicitly the contexts within which harassment is more likely to occur, to avoid victim blame. Our comments will explore the ways in which sexual harassment may be viewed as appropriate behavior for men within the context of typical patterns of socialization by members of institutions, particularly universities, in this society. In addition, the responses of women to harassment will be explored within the context of their socialization by these same institutions.

Organizational Socialization

In his description of the acquisition of work behaviors, Van-Maanen (1976) describes organizational socialization as the process by which a person learns the values, norms and required behaviors which permit participation as a member of an organization. Organizational socialization is portrayed as a process by which individuals develop acceptable values and behaviors, with serious negative consequences for noncompliance. The values of the organization must ultimately be accepted, or dismissal results.

Not all behaviors of employees are as closely monitored by the organization as are others. Schein (1968) differentiates three sets of role behaviors in terms of their centrality to the organization's goals. First, pivotal behaviors include task-related actions, central to the organization's mission, which an individual must perform at a minimally acceptable level. For the university faculty member these would include teaching undergraduate or graduate courses, maintaining an active research program, and serving on university committees. Socialization processes are most concerned with insuring a new member's acceptance of these behaviors. Second, socialization processes may also introduce or make salient certain "relevant" role-behaviors. These behaviors are thought to be desirable but not essential for organizational participation. Standards for the quality of relationships among employees fall into this category—faculty are encouraged to develop collegial relationships with peers. Finally, socialization processes may make salient certain "peripheral" role behaviors which are undesirable, and seen as interfering with achievement of organizational goals. Such behaviors, such as the formation of intimate relationships with students by faculty, may be reinforced by certain segments of the institution; ultimately, though they are destructive.

Such a model of socialization suggests that individuals learn the norms for all acceptable behavior within an organization either directly or indirectly through the process of socialization. Support for such a suggestion is provided by the prevalence of harassment in the workplace and the lack of intervention, or what often appears to be minimal intervention, on the part of some institutions when sexual harassment is documented. In a case involving the former president of the William Mitchell College of Law, for example, eight women who brought suit against the school said that they were each offered about $4,000 if they would sign an agreement retracting their charges. In addition, the defendant's resignation agreement provided for payment of salary and additional benefits, and allowed for his return to the school as a tenured professor (*New York Times*, March 23, 1984).

With this lack of support for victims, it becomes clear that harassing actions are among the behaviors which employees are socialized to believe are acceptable to some segments of organizations. If such behaviors were not reinforced by the institution, they would not continue without sanction. In order to understand the apparent acceptability of harassing behaviors in many organizations it is important to look at the ways in which relationships between men and women in organizations are understood as well as the different perspectives that are held on harassment.

The Nature of Relationships in Organizations

That relationships with co-workers are valued more by women than by men has been documented by a number of researchers (Dubin et al., 1976; Nieva and Gutek, 1981). Women appear to routinely see the development of meaningful relationships as part of a group of pivotal work role behaviors. Men, on the other hand, because they appear to value different aspects of work than women do, do not see the formation of relationships as quite so pivotal work role behaviors. However, they might see the formation of sexual relationships with women as appropriate role-relevant behaviors if socialization within the organization prescribed the formation of sex-role stereotypic relationships among employees. In historically or traditionally male occupations, and in other institutions in which women are represented only in token numbers, such as on university faculties, men and women are likely to interact in sex-role stereotypic ways. Both Kanter (1977) and Gutek and Morasch (1982) have observed this dynamic. Gutek and Morasch suggest that women in nontraditional jobs are seen as women first and work-role occupants second, and as a result report a high frequency of social-sexual behaviors that are not a part of the job. This means that in male-dominated institutions, like most universities, a high frequency of male-dominated social-sexual interactions among men and women would be expected. It is also expected that these interactions would be seen as pivotal behaviors by women and as role-relevant behaviors by men. In traditionally female occupations, women also behave in traditionally sex-typed ways because of sex-role spillover (Gutek and Morasch, 1982), a situation in which gender-based roles which are inappropriate to work carry over into the workplace. Again, a high frequency of relationships characterized by presumptions of male sexual prerogative would be expected.

It is only in sex-balanced organizations that a lower frequency of harassing relationships would be expected, because of less demand for men and women to behave in sex-stereotypic ways.

Gender Differences in the Construction of Social Reality

Linenberger (1983) states:

> Studies reveal that there is a wide divergence of perceptions as to
> what words or actions should result in liability for sexual harass-
> ment. Employers and employees are aware that two well inten-
> tioned people could thoroughly misread each other's signals. What
> one person intends or views as a compliment might be classified by
> another as sexual harassment. People are confused and unsure of
> what is acceptable or unacceptable in their individual relations
> with business colleagues. (p. 238)

Although Linenberger's comments may be taken as indicative of
widespread disagreements on what constitutes harassment distrib-
uted in random fashion across the population, these differences
break down in rather consistent patterns. Gutek[1] and other researchers have consistently noted differences between men and
women in their evaluation of the propriety of sexual attention in
the workplace.

Gender differences in perceptions of the same behavior seem
well established by the time of adolescence. Commenting on conflicting perceptions of the intentions of male and female adolescents
in dating relationships, Zellman et al.[2] suggest that " . . . female adolescents tend to have a less sexualized view of the world than their
male peers. They attribute less sexual meaning to a range of stimuli
in social situations . . . female behaviors innocently performed may
be assumed by male partners to have a sexual meaning." (p. 13)

Among adults, the pattern may continue. "Men do in some circumstances mistake friendliness for seduction. In fact, the whole issue of sexual availability appears to be more salient for men than for
women" (Abbey, 1982). Gutek has noted also that males were more
likely than females to see women as flattered by sexual attention in
the workplace. She reported that men were also significantly more
likely to feel flattered if propositioned than were women. Tangri,
Burt, and Johnson (1982) noted in their survey that for each kind of
harassing behavior about which respondents were asked, more
women than men said that the behavior would bother them and that
they would view it as harassing. They state; "Women, who are four
times as likely to be victims as men, also view sexual harassment
more negatively, and in general are more likely to feel that sexual
behavior and work don't mix" (p. 52). Jensen and Gutek (1982) also

observe that men are more likely than women to blame women for being sexually harassed.

These differences in the perception of harassment appear consistent with more general differences in perceptions of social reality described by Gilligan and others. In describing problems in marital relationships, for example, Gilligan[3] has suggested that men and women share an overlapping moral vocabulary, but attach different meanings to its words. Two well-publicized cases of sexual harassment provide examples of this. In the first, the defendant suggested that "the tone of the conversation was not meant to be offensive" (*New York Times*, June 1, 1982). In the other the defendant stated that "normal, affectionate pats on the shoulder were misinterpreted by the women" (*New York Times*, March 23, 1984). In response to appeals from women to right the injustice come claims of misunderstanding and exaggerated sensitivity.

Clearly, if one invokes an ethic of rights in which justice is defined by notions of reciprocity, the ethic which Gilligan (1977,1982) and others have tied more closely to male development, then men who report that they would be flattered by sexual attention in the workplace are not disposed to view such attention to a woman as harassment. However, the judgment of what is just and fair based on placing the self in the role of other fails to recognize the differences in perception of sexual behavior just noted, as well as common power differentials. Men who believe that they would be flattered by such attention were the situation reversed, employ a logic of fairness rather than the logic of relationships and connectedness which Gilligan has identified as more associated with women's judgments of morality. Lyons (1983) in particular has suggested that since women are more likely to define individuals as connected in relation to others, those others are seen in their own situations and contexts. The morality of care then rests on relationships as responses to others on their terms. The observation that some women are likely to remain within harassing relationships because they do not want to hurt their harassers (Livingston, 1982), and because they generally perceive relationships as protective (Pollak and Gilligan, 1982) is much more comprehensible when one adopts such a perspective. We[4] have suggested elsewhere that because women have not shared equally in the development of norms for interaction in many organizations, the prevailing morality of most institutions is more characterized by what may be termed male values. This dominant institutional "morality" or ethic is one based on respect for the autonomy of individuals, and for the integrity of people as separate from those around them. A claim as to the inviolability of "academic freedom" in universities represents such an ethic. Justice is predicated on the responsibility of individuals acting within reciprocal relationships, and guarantee of individual rights (Lyons, 1983).

The occurrence and maintenance of sexual harassment within major institutions may now be understood within a framework which suggests that competing moralities are likely to perpetuate such behaviors. By virtue of sex segregation of jobs, institutions support stereotypic relations among men and women, and socialize members with such expectations. Because there is typically a lack of understanding between men and women about what a common set of behaviors mean and a difference in perspectives on the centrality of relationships in the work environment, conflict is likely to result. When conflict does result, the institution is likely to provide support for an articulation of work role behaviors that is consistent with definitions of the group that is more present in positions of control. In 1980, Susan Meyer, Executive Director of the Working Women's Institute, suggested that among employers there was still some feeling that sexual harassment was titillating, or that it was a joke. It was only when employers were told that it was an employment problem which affected their pocketbooks and productivity that harassment was taken seriously (*New York Times*, October 24, 1980). We would suggest that harassment continues to remain a problem because it is sanctioned by organizations through socialization of new employees, and because the dominant ethic of organizations is one which maintains the sanctity of the individual male rights of dominance. Women perpetuate harassment only insofar as they value the centrality of satisfying relationships with co-workers at their own expense.

Hoffman (1986) suggests that

> institutions seriously interested in elimination of the causes of sexual harassment, as well as its behavioral manifestations, must apply theory to practice. The transformation potential of integrating the recent scholarship on women into the curriculum; of increasing the numbers, status and authority of women staff and faculty on college campuses; and of challenging bureaucratic forms of domination and subordination through organized resistance to centralized authority and depersonalized control remains a vision of what could be, a vision which should inform discourse about the responses to sexual harassment on college campuses.

That we cannot leave transformation of university socializing agents to those whose judgments are uninformed by the results of feminist scholarship on sexual harassment is made clear by Fitzgerald and her colleagues (1988). In looking at the understanding male faculty have the nature of their social and sexual interactions with female students, Fitzgerald identified a number of ways in which the faculty denied the power differential which exists between themselves and female students. Respondents to their survey believed in the possibility of mutual consent, even when members of a dyad differed significantly in status and influence within the academic institution. Belief in such mutuality would lead to blaming of the female student if she experienced negative consequences of the relationship, an outcome with a high probability, given Reid and Robinson's findings.

We would suggest that the perspective we have developed, one which grows out of feminist scholarship, should be integrated into sexual harassment policies, as well as into curricula. The numbers, status and authority of women faculty, staff and students should be increased on college campuses. And bureaucratic forms of domination and subordination should be supplanted by alternative decision-making structures, which empower women who have traditionally been excluded from policy making. Some of the interventions that we have discussed, achieve these ends, and we'd like to spend some time discussing the ways in which various programs reflect basic changes in traditional patterns of domination and subordination.

Notes

1. B. Gutek (1981). Experiences of sexual harassment: Results from a representative survey. In S. Tangri (Chair), Sexual harassment at work: Evidence, remedies and implications. Paper presented at the meeting of the American Psychological Association, Los Angeles.

2. G. L. Zellman, Johnson P. B., Giarusso, R., & Goodchilds, J. D. (1979). Adolescent expectations for dating relationships: Consensus and conflict between the sexes. Paper presented at the meeting of the American Psychological Association, New York.

3. C. Gilligan. (1982). Marital dialogues. Paper presented at the conference, "Developing through Relationships," University of Kansas, Lawrence.

4. A. Fuehrer, & K. M. Schilling. (1984). The values of organizations. Paper presented at the meeting of the American Psychological Association (Division 35, Open Symposium), Toronto.

References

Abbey, A. (1982). Sex differences in attributions for friendly behavior: Do males misperceive females' friendliness? *Journal of Personality and Social Psychology, 42,* 830–38.

Dubin, R., Hedley, R. A., & Taveggia, T. C. (1976). Attachment to work. In R. Dubin (Ed.), *Handbook of work, organization and society.* Chicago: Rand McNally, 281–341.

Dziech, B. W., & Weiner, L. (1984). *The lecherous professor: Sexual harassment on campus.* Boston: Beacon Press.

Fitzgerald, L. F., Weitzman, L. M., Gold, Y., & Ormerod, M. (1988). Academic harassment: Sex and denial in scholarly garb. *Psychology of Women Quarterly, 12,* 329–40.

Gilligan, C. (1977). In a different voice: Women's conceptions of self and morality. *Harvard Educational Review, 47,* 481–517.

Gilligan, C. (1982). *In a Different Voice.* Cambridge: Harvard University Press.

Goodman, J. L. (1978). Sexual harassment on the job. *American Civil Liberties Review, 4*(6), 55–58.

Gutek, B., & Morasch, B. (1982). Sex-ratios, sex-role spillover, and sexual harassment of women at work. *Journal of Social Issues, 38,* 55–74.

Hoffman, F. L. (1986). Sexual harassment in academia: Feminist theory and institutional practice. *Harvard Educational Review, 56,* 105–21.

Jensen, I., & Gutek, B. (1982). Attributions and assignment of responsibility for sexual harassment. *Journal of Social Issues, 38,* 121–36

Kanter, R. M. (1977). *Men and women of the corporation.* New York: Basic Books.

Linenberger, P. (1983). What behavior constitutes sexual harassment? *Labor Law Journal, 34,* 238–47.

Livingston, J. (1982). Responses to sexual harassment on the job: Legal, organizational and individual actions. *Journal of Social Issues, 38,* 5–22.

Lyons, N. P. (1983). Two perspectives: On self, relationships, and morality. *Harvard Educational Review, 53,*

New York Times. Minnesota law school sued in a sexual harassment case. March 23, 1984, B, 18, 5.

New York Times. Sexual harassment at work: A sensitive and confusing issue. October 24, 1980, A20.

New York Times. Teacher to offer to leave his post. June 1, 1982, A, 18, 3.

Nieva, V., & Gutek, B. (1981). *Women and work: A psychological perspective.* New York: Praeger.

Pollak, S., & Gilligan, C. (1982). Images of violence in Thematic Apperception Test stories. *Journal of Personality and Social Psychology, 42,* 159–67.

Russell, D. (1984). *Sexual exploitation: Rape, child sexual abuse and workplace harassment.* Beverly Hills, Calif.: Sage.

Schein, E. (1968). Organizational socialization. *Industrial Management Review, 2,* 37–45.

Tangri, S., Burt, M., & Johnson L. (1982). Sexual harassment at work: Three explanatory models. *Journal of Social Issues, 38,* 33–54.

VanMaanen, J. (1976). Breaking in: Socialization to work. In R. Dubin (Ed.), *Handbook of work, organization and society.* Chicago: Rand McNally, 67–130.

The Stress Effects of Sexual Harassment on the Job

By Peggy Crull, New York Commission on Human Rights, formerly of Working Women's Institute. Reprinted here with permission.

Introduction

Sexual harassment has always been part of the experience of women who worked outside their own homes. Sexual intrusions such as lewd comments, inappropriate touching, propositions, and even rape have been described in historical accounts of the daily work life of women, but they were not singled out for analysis as a social phenomenon until recently.[1,3] In the mid-1970s these experiences were given a name, brought to public attention, and recognized as a barrier to women's full participation in the work force.[9,18] Early publicity focused on the fact that women often were fired or had to resign from jobs when they refused to comply with the sexual demands of their bosses. The research which followed was aimed primarily at determining the incidence of sexual harassment.[4,7,8,14,15]

Working Women's Institute's contact with thousands of women who have encountered this problem indicates that in addition to its well-publicized economic repercussions, sexual harassment has effects on its victims which are of concern to mental health professionals.[5] Women who come to the Institute for information, referral, and counseling often react to the sexual harassment dilemma with stress symptoms such as excessive tension and health problems. In many cases their productivity, enjoyment of work, and overall sense of well-being are impaired. With the increase in public awareness about sexual harassment, mental health practitioners will be faced with more and more women in this situation and will need to understand these often-hidden stress effects. The following is an analysis of case material gathered from clients of Working Women's Institute's Information, Referral, and Counseling Service. It will describe typical sexual harassment situations and reactions to them, attempt to explain the reactions, and draw implications for counseling sexual harassment victims.

Method

Study Population

The case material which will be discussed comes from two sources. (1) Late in 1978, we mailed questionnaires to 325 women who had written us for assistance between 1975 and 1978. The questionnaire asked for information on the woman's age, occupation, and marital status at the time of the harassment experience. Respondents were asked to describe their experience and any effects it had on their job performance, psychological well-being, and physical health. Ninety-two completed questionnaires, or about 28% of those sent out were returned and used in the analysis. (2) The second source of material is records kept on clients of the Institute's crisis counseling service. Except for occupation and description of the sexual harassment situation, the information contained in the mailed questionnaire is not necessarily asked for or recorded in counseling sessions. However, much of that information arises spontaneously in the sessions and is noted in the counselor's records. The present analysis uses records of the 170 clients who had complete counseling sessions at the Institute between February and December of 1979.

Date Analysis

The open-ended material from the questionnaire and clients' records was subjected to a content analysis and codes were developed. The areas covered by these codes were occupation, type of harassment, and effect of harassment on job performance, psychological well-being, and physical health. The data from the questionnaires and clients records was combined for the analyses, except where there is a large discrepancy in the results. Except where otherwise indicated, therefore, the results are based on 262 women.

Results

Demographic Information

The age range of the women in the sample is 16 to 65 years. About 20% of the sample consists of minority women. The women who mailed back the questionnaire are from all parts of the United

States, while the counseling clients are concentrated in the New York Metropolitan area. The distribution of occupations in the sample is similar to that of all working women, although clerical workers are more heavily represented in our sample (see Fig. 1). Women in this sample work in almost every sector of the economy and in every type of industry.

Fig. 1. Occupational Distribution of the Sample (Questionnaire Respondents and Clients Combined)

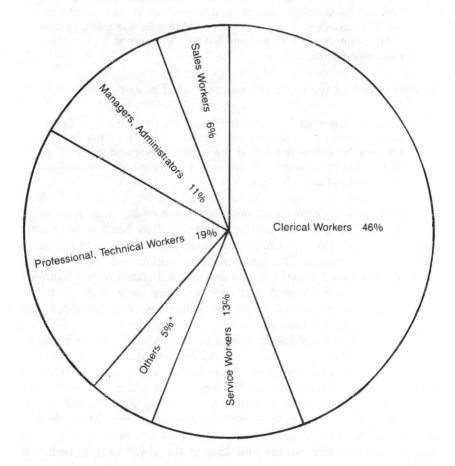

* "Others" includes Craft Workers; Operatives; Transport Equipment Operatives; Laborers (non-farm); Private Household Workers; and Farm Workers.

Types of Sexual Harassment

The most common mode of sexual harassment was verbal—repeated comments about the woman's body, jokes about her sexual behavior, and sexual propositions. About half of the group was subjected to physical advances such as touching and kissing. Verbal and physical contact involved sexual parts of the body like the breasts. In about a fifth of all the cases the sexual advances were accompanied by some stated threat to the woman's job.

> He would call me into his office for no reason and just talk about how bad his marriage was. He said he couldn't stand to work near me if I wouldn't go to bed with him and that he was going to have to let me go. Sometimes he even left little presents as bribes which I always returned.[1]

In almost 20% of the cases the harasser used physical force.

> It started out with just comments and then propositions. Sometimes he would try to grab me from behind or grab my breasts. One day he followed me into the storage closet and grabbed me and started to unbutton my uniform. He twisted my arm so hard that I couldn't move it the next day.

In about four-fifths of all the cases the harasser was a superior who had the authority to fire the woman or deny her a raise or promotion directly. The remaining 20% were co-workers, subordinates, customers, or clients. The questionnaire respondents (but not the clients) were asked about the age and marital status of the harasser and the responses showed that the harassers were likely to be in their mid-40s and married while the women were in their 30s and single, divorced or widowed.

Over two-thirds of the women were subjected to apparent retaliation when they refused to accede to the sexual advances or innuendoes. They were refused promotions, kept out of training programs, and denied letters of reference. In some instances their work was criticized unduly and they were held up for professional and personal ridicule before subordinates or clients. More than a quarter of the women had been fired or laid off. Forty-two percent of the questionnaire sample and 25% of the client sample resigned

---

[1] In order to assure confidentiality, all quotes used in this paper are adaptations or composites of statements from people in the sample.

from their jobs because of the sexual harassment or the "work harassment" which accompanied it.

Reactions to Sexual Harassment

Whether or not they lost their jobs, almost all of the women experienced debilitating stress reactions as a result of the sexual and work harassment. We divided these stress effects into three categories: (1) effects on work performance, (2) effects on general psychological well-being, and (3) effects on physical health. Figure 2 shows

Fig. 2. Percentage of Sample Reporting Various Stress Effects (Questionnaire Respondents and Clients Combined).

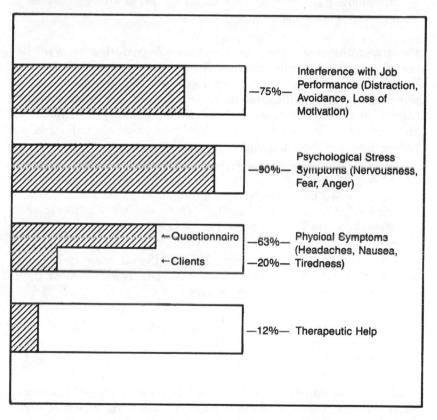

---

*The stress effects listed in parentheses are the most commonly mentioned in each category.

the percentage of subjects who reported stress effects of each of those three types and the major symptoms which were included in each category.

Although many of our subjects expressed pride at being able to do their jobs despite the difficult situation, 75% of them conceded that their job performance had suffered. The most common complaint was that they could not concentrate on their work because of the presence of sexual innuendoes. A large number of women tried to avoid them altogether by taking sick days or trying to confine their work to locations away from the harasser.

> I would not go into the computer center and work with him alone. Sometimes this wasted my time since I needed to work early in the morning when no one else was there but him.

In a large number of cases, the effect on job performance went beyond the immediate situation and women found that their motivation to work was waning. They reported that they became unsure of their skills and accomplishments in the face of the retaliation and criticism that followed their refusal to be sexually available. For some, the blow to their self-confidence was great enough to cause them to doubt if they had chosen the right career.

> It gave me the feeling that any initiative I took would be futile. They implied that I wouldn't get a promotion unless I was "cooperative." After awhile, I thought "Maybe I'm really not creative enough. Maybe I should get out of advertising."

About 90% of the women reported that the situation had caused them some kind of psychological stress. The reaction most often mentioned was general tension or nervousness.

> When this started happening, I became very nervous. It made me emotionally upset all the time. I hated to go to work. Finally, my doctor put me on tranquilizers.

In addition, the situation often aroused anger and fear—the anger at the unjust treatment and the fear from not knowing where to turn.

> I was paralyzed. I couldn't think or act because I was afraid. I thought people would belittle me, say I was imagining it. It turned

out I was right. People at the Human Relations Division said there was nothing I could do about it. That was the last straw!

Sixty-three percent of the women who answered the questionnaire and 20% of the counseling clients pointed out physical symptoms they thought had been brought on by their dilemma. The most prevalent forms of physical distress were nausea, headaches, and tiredness.

> Even the smallest job seemed like too much effort. I began having headaches and crying at the slightest problem. I really knew something was wrong when I had an accident driving to work for the night shift. I ran a light, something I'd never done before.

Frequently the women did not connect their physical disturbances with the sexual harassment until the situation changed and the symptom disappeared. A number of them (about 12%) had sought the help of a doctor or psychotherapist to alleviate their psychological and physical distress.

Discussion

This case material gives us a picture of the dynamics and effects of sexual harassment which provides a framework for crisis counseling with women who have undergone this trauma. The kinds of advances encountered by the present sample are intrusive and coercive behaviors which not only irritate and embarrass, but also threaten the woman's job security and violate her physical privacy. The harassment often does not stop with sexual suggestions, touches or propositions but is transformed into work harassment such as undue criticism of work performance, humiliation in front of co-workers, refusal to give positive references. In a substantial number of cases the end result is firing or denial of promotions or raises. This situation causes noticeable stress, whether or not it leads to a measurable financial setback or job loss. It creates feelings of anger, fear, and worthlessness which interfere not only with work performance and aspirations, but also with psychological and physical health. Sexual harassment, then, is similar to other occupational health hazards like speed-up or poor lighting in that it drains women's energy, damages their health, and ultimately reduces their earning power often without their realizing it.[16] These results raise at least three questions which will be the focus of the remainder of the discussion.

(1) The first question is whether or not these experiences and reactions are typical for victims of sexual harassment. Several large mail surveys on sexual harassment which have been conducted over the last five years confirm the patterns of harassment incidents we have described here. As in our sample, the form of harassment most commonly reported in the surveys is verbal, and physical harassment also occurs in a substantial number of cases.[4,7,14,18] Those that inquired about work harassment uncovered a range of incidents similar to those we have reported.[8,11,15] None of the surveys explored stress effects and effects on work performance, although some found that women react to sexual harassment with anger, fear, and nervousness.[4,14,18] To date there are no published reports of clinical research which might provide more detailed data on the dynamics and effects of sexual harassment.

Because the women in our sample have sought specific help, they probably differ in several ways from the survey participants and sexual harassment victims in general. Their experiences are probably more serious than those of the general population. For example, women whose situations are resolved quickly and without extensive repercussions are not as likely to write for help or seek counseling. We can speculate that they do not experience the high level of stress found in our sample. On the other hand, many women too isolated to know where to turn, or too ashamed to talk to anyone about their experience probably do not contact us. We have heard of cases in which women, desperate to hold onto their jobs and unaware of any alternatives have submitted unwillingly to sexual advances, sometimes including intercourse, for a period of months or years without telling even their closest friends. This situations undoubtedly leads to more severe reactions than those we have described in our sample. It should also be noted that our sample does not include women who have been engaged in mutual sexual behavior such as reciprocal flirting, dating, or an affair that has been agreed upon by both parties and which had no negative consequences for their work. There is no reason such women would seek help. Our sample does include several cases of women who became targets of work harassment or received disparate or discriminatory treatment after a mutual relationship with a boss or supervisor ended.

(2) A second question which grows out of these results is: Why are stress symptoms, and loss of motivation and self-confidence common reactions among women to sexual harassment? A look at the position of women in the work force provides the overall frame-

work for answering this question. Despite the influx of women into the labor force, statistics show that women generally hold lower status jobs than those held by most men.[17] They are more likely than men to be in jobs which require minimal formal education or training and are, thus, more replaceable than the men in their workplace. Therefore, there is a high probability that the man who directs his sexual attentions toward a woman has certain advantages over her. He is likely to be in a position of direct or indirect authority over her job. If he does not officially have authority, he probably has seniority or is better trained or better acquainted with the men in supervisory positions. Even if he is a co-worker, there is a good possibility that he is responsible for training her, especially if she is in a traditionally male field such as construction work.

Given these circumstances, the woman faced with sexual harassment must decide how to handle it based on the knowledge that her job could be in jeopardy. But choosing a strategy is made difficult by cultural norms with spect to male and female sexuality. In our culture sexual aggression is seen as an important element of masculinity. Men are thought to have a right and even responsibility to pursue a woman aggressively.[12,13] The woman who directly refuses or complains about the sexual advances appears to be challenging this right. Sensing that the harasser could fight back through work harassment, she hesitates to take this course. On the other hand, the woman who tried to save the harasser's ego and her job by ignoring or politely handling the advances may be trapped by a related cultural norm which says that women are supposed to show their interest in men in an indirect manner.[13] Harassers often interpret the woman's attempts to be diplomatic as a discreet "yes" or as an invitation to try harder. In a 1975 survey conducted by Working Women's Institute, 75% of the women who tried to ignore sexual advances at work found that they escalated.[18] In many cases, trying to handle or ignore the advances leads to retaliation in the same way that objecting to them does when the harasser realizes the woman is not reciprocating. Therefore, the woman is in a double bind. If she directly refuses or objects to the sexual attention she risks job security or advancement. If she tries to ignore or politely handle it, it will continue and very likely get more intense or result in job loss anyway. The conflict created by this double bind expresses itself as mental and physical stress symptoms.

The problem of the double bind is complicated by other aspects of sexual socialization. Girl's education to male sexuality includes the message that they are responsible for controlling male sexual behavior. The woman who becomes the target of sexual attention at work may feel guilty that she in some way caused the behavior.[12] Many of the women in our sample pondered endlessly over what they could have done to halt the situation, feeling that they should have realized what was going on, or that they should have been less friendly at work altogether. Indeed, it is often suggested that women cause sexual harassment by the way they dress and act.[2] The feeling of guilt created by these attitudes may make it harder for the woman to speak up and increases the likelihood that she will internalize the problem.

Another complication is created by the belief that women should put their families before their jobs, even when their earnings are essential to family security. When a situation of sexual harassment arises it serves as a jarring reminder to the woman that she may have overstepped her bounds and risked her family's well-being by working outside the home. We have found that women caught in a sexual harassment dilemma frequently meet with an "I told you so" from a spouse or parents who feel that they should devote themselves solely to home and children. Losing ambition and interest in work appears in cases like this to be an almost unconscious resolution of this problem.

The reactions we have observed make sense in light of what we know about women's self-esteem with respect to intellectual and related abilities. They do not expect to do well in school and are not confident about predicting their performance at such tasks as anagrams.[10] When they perform well at a task, they tend to attribute their success to chance, whereas they feel poor performance is their fault.[6] In the sexual harassment situation, women's difficulty in judging their own abilities is exacerbated by the criticism of their work that we have labeled work harassment and by their diminished performance in the face of stress. They begin to lose self-confidence because they attribute these problems to their own lack of skill rather than external circumstances.

(3) Finally, this study raises the question of how to approach counseling victims of sexual harassment. The results and interpretations suggest an approach. Because stress symptoms and diminished interest in work, and waning self-confidence appear to be common in this situation, they should be treated in most instances as situational reactions rather than individual pathologies. The major function of counseling, then, is to help the woman understand her reactions and work through her feelings so that she can make realistic decisions about how to resolve her situation. The counselor

will need to create an atmosphere in which the woman will feel free to explore and vent her feelings of anger, guilt, and inadequacy. The counselor may also need to help the woman make connections between stress symptoms and her job situations. Armed with a knowledge of the dynamics of the situation and her own reactions to it the woman will be in a better position to try to save her job, look for a new job, seek unemployment, or take some legal action.

This paper only touches on some of the major issues which must be understood in the sexual harassment situation. It does not attempt to cover any of the concrete coping strategies or legal information that the counselor can provide for the client, but these certainly should be included in crisis intervention work with sexual harassment victims. In addition, more research is needed to delineate the variables which create the kinds of stress we have described and to explore other ramifications of the sexual harassment situation.

References

1. Alcott, L. M. 1894. How I went out to service. The Independent (New York) (1331).

2. Berns, W. 1980. (October). Terms of endearment, Harpers. 261 (1565): 14+.

3. Bularzik, M. 1978. Sexual harassment at the workplace: Historical notes. Radical America. 12(4): 24–43.

4. Carey, S. 1977. Sexual politics in business. Paper presented at the Southwestern Social Science Association. Dallas, Texas.

5. Crull, P. 1979. The impact of sexual harassment on the job: A profile of the experiences of 92 women. In D. Neugarten and J. Shafritz (Eds.) Sexuality in Organizations: Romantic and Coercive Behaviors at Work. Oak Park, Illinois: Moore Publishing Company: 67–71.

6. Deaux, K. 1976. The Behavior of Women and Men. Monterey, California: Brooks/Cole Publishing Company.

7. Hayler, B. 1980. Testimony before the House Judiciary II Committee, State of Illinois.

8. Largen, M. 1979. Report on sexual harassment in federal employment. New Responses, Inc. Bethesda, Md.

9. Lindsey, K. 1977. (November). Sexual harassment on the job and how to stop it. Ms. XI (5): 47+.

10. Maccoby, E. 1974. The Psychology of Sex Differences. Stanford: Stanford University Press.

11. Merit Systems Protection Board. 1980. Summary of preliminary findings on sexual harassment in the federal workplace given before the subcommittee on investigations committee on post office and civil service, U.S. House of Representatives.

12. Phelps, L. 1979. Female sexual alienation. In Jo Freeman (Ed.) Women: A Feminist Perspective. Palo Alto, California: Mayfield Publishing Company: 18–26.

13. Rosenbaum, M. 1976. Clarity of the seduction situation. In J. Wiseman (Ed.) The Sociology of Sex. New York: Harper and Row: 50–57.

14. Safron, C. 1976. What men do to women on the job. Redbook.

15. Sexual harassment rampant at HUD. 1979. Impact Journal. VII (11 and 12).

16. Stellman, J. 1977. Women's Work, Women's Health. New York: Vintage Books.

17. U.S. Department of Labor, Employment Standards Administration, Women's Bureau. 1979. The earnings gap between women and men.

18. Working Women's Institute. 1975. Sexual harassment on the job: Results of a preliminary survey. Research Series, Report Number 1.

Sexual Harassment of Students: Victims of the College Experience

By Michele Paludi and Richard Barickman. Reprinted with permission from the authors.

Sexual harassment in U.S. colleges and universities is a major barrier to women's professional development and a traumatic force that disrupts and damages their personal lives (Betz & Fitzgerald, 1987). Dziech and Weiner (1984) have reported that 30% of undergraduate women suffer sexual harassment from at least one of their instructors during their four years of college. When definitions of sexual harassment include sexist remarks and other forms of "gender harassment," the incidence rate in undergraduate populations nears 70% (Adams, Kottke, Padgitt 1983; Lott, Reilly, & Howard, 1982). These percentages translate into millions of students in our college system who are sexually harassed each year. The incidence rate for women graduate students and faculty is even higher (Bailey & Richards, 1985; Bond, 1988). Though there are few studies focusing on the sexual harassment of nonfaculty employees in the college/ university system, there is no reason to suppose that the harassment of college staff is any less than the 50% rate reported for employees of various other public and private institutions (Fitzgerald, Shullman, Bailey, Richards, Swecker, Gold, Ormerod, & Weitzman, 1988). Sexual harassment is thus a major form of victimization of women in our system of higher education, even though it is still largely a "hidden issue" (as the Project on the Status and Education of Women called it in 1978).

Women students and faculty who have been harassed often change their entire educational program as a result. And, stress reactions—often severe—almost invariably follow sexual harassment, including depression, tension, anger and fear, insomnia, headaches, feelings of helplessness, and embarrassment, and decreased motivation (Whitmore, 1983). Performance in course work suffers, and many students drop out of school altogether.

We propose in this study to (1) review the psychological literature that documents the impact of harassment; (2) describe the differing perceptions of sexual harassment commonly held by women and men; and (3) offer suggestions for curtailing sexual harassment through the institution of college policies and panels to enforce them, training of faculty and graduate students, and educational campaigns to inform the academic community of the nature and severity of the problem.

Although our particular focus will be on the victimization of students, the circumstances we describe and remedies we propose apply to faculty and staff as well. If the awareness of the nature of sexual harassment—especially the severe damage it inflicts on women—is increased within the academic community, and if remedial action is taken, all members of the community will benefit (including potential and actual harassers).

Definitions and Incidence of Sexual Harassment

The nature, range, and impact of sexual harassment in college/university settings may be suggested by the words of the victims themselves (as quoted in a pamphlet prepared by the U.S. Department of Education's Office for Civil Rights):

> I was discussing my work in a public setting when a professor cut me off and asked if I had freckles all over my body.

> He (the teaching assistant) kept saying, don't worry about the grade, and you know we'll settle everything out of class.

> I see male colleagues and professors chum it up and hear all the talk about making the old boy network operate for women, so I thought nothing of accepting an invitation from a . . . professor to attend a gathering at his house. Other graduate students were present. . . . The professor made a fool out of himself pursuing me (it took me a while to catch on) and then blurted, "You know I want to sleep with you; I have a great deal of influence. Now, of course I don't want to force you into anything, but I'm sure you're going to be sensible about this." I fled.

Playboy centerfolds were used as Anatomy teaching slides. . . . In slides, lectures, teaching aids and even our own student note service, we found that nurses were presented as sexy, bitchy, or bossy but never as professional health care workers.

The financial officer made it clear that I could get the money I needed if I slept with him.

Women experience sexual harassment in many forms—from sexist remarks and covert physical contact (patting and brushing against their bodies) to blatant propositions and sexual assaults. Researchers have developed five categories to encompass the range of sexual harassment (Fitzgerald et al., 1988): gender harassment, seductive behavior, sexual bribery, sexual coercion, and sexual imposition. These levels of sexual harassment correlate with legal definitions of sexual harassment.

Gender harassment consists of generalized sexist remarks and behavior not designed to elicit sexual cooperation but rather to convey insulting, degrading, or sexist attitudes about women. *Seductive behavior* is unwanted, inappropriate, and offensive sexual advances. *Sexual bribery* is the solicitation of sexual activity or other sex-linked behavior by threat of punishment, and *sexual imposition* includes gross sexual imposition, assault, and rape.

Sexual harassment is clearly prohibited within the college/university system as a form of sexual discrimination, under both Title IX of the 1972 Education Amendments and, for employees, Title VII of the 1964 Civil Rights Act. A key definition of sexual harassment has been issued by the Education Department's Office of Civil Rights (OCR):

Sexual harassment consists of verbal or physical conduct of a sexual nature, imposed on the basis of sex, by an employee or agent of a recipient of federal funds that denies, limits, provides different, or conditions the provision of aid, benefits, services, or treatment protected under Title IX.

In addition, guidelines first issued by the Equal Employment Opportunity Commission (interpreting Title VII) and adopted in 1981 by the OCR further specify the range of sexual harassment covered by these statutes. According to these guidelines, behavior constitutes sexual harassment when:

The person engaging in such behavior explicitly or implicitly makes your submission to it a term or condition of your employment or academic standing.

The person engaging in such behavior makes decisions affecting your employment or academic life according to whether you accept or reject that behavior.

The person's behavior is an attempt to interfere, or has the effect of interfering, with your work or academic performance, or creates an intimidating, hostile, or offensive working or learning environment.

The last condition—the creation of "an intimidating, hostile, or offensive working or learning environment"—is particularly significant because it covers the most pervasive form of sexual harassment, the form most often defended on the grounds of "academic freedom." In a 1986 decision, *Meritor Savings Bank v. Vinson*, the Supreme Court unanimously affirmed that "sexual harassment claims are not limited simply to those for which a tangible job benefit is withheld ('quid pro quo' sexual harassment), but also includes those in which the complainant is subjected to an offensive, discriminatory work environment ('hostile environment' sexual harassment)" (Bennett-Alexander, 1987, 65). In doing so the Court explicitly adopted the EEOC's guidelines, which have been extended to the academic community—especially to students, who are not covered by the statutes governing employer/employee relations—by the OCR. These guidelines thus have a regulating force supported by the U.S. Department of Education that is crucial to the effort to curtail the widespread sexual harassment now afflicting our colleges and universities.

In response to the decision in *Vinson*, and in the spirit of this effort, the American Council on Education issued the following statement to all its members in December, 1986:

Although the *Vinson* decision applies specifically to employment, it is prudent to examine the case and its implications for the campus setting. This provides an opportunity to renew institutional commitment to eliminating sexual harassment, or to develop an institution-wide program to address the problem. . . .

The educational mission of a college or university is to foster an open learning and working environment. The ethical obligation to provide an environment that is free from sexual harassment and from the fear that it may occur is implicit. The entire collegiate community suffers when sexual harassment is allowed to pervade the academic atmosphere through neglect, the lack of a policy prohibiting it, or the lack of educational programs designed to clarify appropriate professional behavior on campus and to promote understanding of what constitutes sexual harassment. Each institution has the obligation, for moral as well as legal reasons, to develop policies, procedures, and programs that protect students and employees from sexual harassment and to establish an environment in which such unacceptable behavior will not be tolerated.

In recent years, research has provided compelling evidence that sexual and gender harassment of students can result in serious psychological, emotional, physical, and economic consequences (Koss, 1990). Such harassment often forces students to forfeit research, work, and even their career plans. Research by Adams, Kottke, and Padgitt (1983) reported that 13% of the women students they surveyed said they had avoided taking a class or working with certain professors because of the risk of being subjected to sexual advances. Furthermore, a 1983 study conducted at Harvard University indicated that 15% of the graduate students and 12% of the undergraduate students who had been harassed by their professors changed their major or educational program because of the harassment. Wilson and Kraus (1983) reported that 9% of the female undergraduates in their study had been pinched, touched, or patted to the point of personal discomfort, while 17% of the women in the Adams, et al. survey received verbal sexual advances, 14% received sexual invitations, 6% had been subjected to physical advances, and 2% received direct sexual bribes.

Bailey and Richards (1985) reported that of 246 women graduate students in their sample, 13% indicated they had been sexually harassed, 21% had not enrolled in a course to avoid such behavior and 16% indicated they had been directly assaulted. Bond (1988) reported that 75% of the 229 women members of Division 27 who responded to her survey experienced jokes with sexual themes during their graduate training, 69% were subjected to sexist comments demeaning to women, and 58% of the women reported experiencing sexist remarks about their clothing, body, or sexual activities.

All of these findings indicate that when definitions of sexual victimization include sexual and gender harassment, it becomes clear that the sexual victimization of women is pervasive: literally millions of women each year experience victimization in the college/ university setting.

Explanatory Models and Institutional Structure

Sexual harassment occurs, in most instances, when individuals exploit a position of power granted to them by their roles in an institutional structure. This is as true for the classroom setting as it is for the workplace. Yet the major impasse to a general acknowledgment that sexual harassment is a devastating force in our educational system probably continues to be the widespread view that this is a matter of personal relations outside the control of the institution and unrelated to its own powers and prerogatives. Zalk (1990) has raised the falseness and insensitivity of this view:

> All the power lies with the faculty member—some of it real, concrete, and some of it is imagined or elusive. The bases of the faculty member's almost absolute power are varied and range from the entirely rational into broad areas of fantasy. Professors give grades, write recommendations for graduate schools, awards and the like, and can predispose colleagues' attitudes towards students.

The idea that sexual harassment is an inherently personal rather than an institutional matter is a variation on the explanatory framework called the "natural/biological model" by Tangri, Burt, and Johnson (1982). They have identified three explanatory models that individuals typically use to account for sexual harassment. The natural/biological model interprets sexual harassment as a consequence of natural sexual interactions between people, either attributing a stronger sex drive to men than to women (thus men "need" to engage in aggressive sexual behavior) or describing sexual harassment as part of the "game" between sexual equals. This model obviously can't account for the extreme stress reactions suffered by victims of sexual harassment (and not suffered by their harassers). It is as fallacious as a racist theory that attributes the victimization of minorities to a "natural" prerogative or capacity of a superior race or to the "inevitable" workings of social forces.

The *sociocultural model* posits sexual harassment as only one manifestation of the much larger patriarchal system in which men are the dominant group. Therefore, harassment is an example of men asserting their personal power based on sex. According to this model, sex would be a better predictor of both recipient and initiator status than would organizational position. Thus, women should be much more likely to be victims of sexual harassment, especially when they are in male-populated college majors.

This model gives a much more accurate account of sexual harassment since the overwhelming majority of victims are women and the overwhelming majority of harassers are men (90–95% in each case; Fitzgerald, et al., 1988). Yet it can have the unfortunate effect of leaving women feeling nearly as powerless as the natural/biological model does. If sexual harassment is so ingrained in our whole culture, how can the individual withstand such a massive, systemic force?

The *organizational model* asserts that sexual harassment results from opportunities presented by relations of power and authority which derive from the hierarchical structure of organizations. Thus, sexual harassment is an issue of organizational power. Since work (and academic) organizations are defined by vertical stratification and asymmetrical relations between supervisors and subordinates, teachers and students, individuals can use the power of their position to extort sexual gratification from their subordinates.

This model is most useful for understanding and opposing sexual harassment in the academy, in our experience. But it should be—to obtain the fullest explanatory range and corrective power—combined with the sociocultural model. Organizational power is so pervasively abused, victimizing literally tens of millions of women in the workplace, schools, colleges, and universities, *because* sexual inequality and victimization are endemic to our patriarchal culture. Just as the frequency of rape in warfare is a consequence of general cultural values licensed by the extreme "organizational structure" of war, so the frequency of sexual harassment is a consequence of these same values empowered by the ordinary, routine structures of work and education. Again, the analogy to racial discrimination holds.

Implications for Education and Policy

Recently, Dovan, Grossman, Kindermann, Matula, Paludi, and Scott (1987) reported that college women were more likely to label a faculty member's harassment of a woman student in terms of his abusing his power as a professor over the student instead of abusing his power as a man. They recognized sexual harassment as allowing professors to undermine students' positions in higher education. This finding supports the organizational model of harassment: women were able to explain harassment as resulting from the opportunities presented by power and authority relations which derive from the hierarchical structure of the academy. This echoes May's (1972) description of power in the academy.

> If we take the university as the setting, we need only ask any graduate student whether his [sic] professors have power over him, and he will laugh at our naïveté. The perpetual anxiety of some graduate students as to whether they will be passed or not is proof enough. The professor's power is even more effective because it is clothed in scholarly garb. It is the power of prestige, status, and the subtle coercions of others that follow from these. (p. 102)

In a 1984 statement to all faculty at Harvard, the Dean of Arts and sciences, Henry Rosovsky reported on the Faculty Council's view of such inequalities in relation to all sexual contacts between students and teachers, the supposedly "consensual" as well as the obviously harassing:

> Amorous relationships that might be appropriate in other circumstances are always wrong when they occur between any teacher or officer of the University and any student for whom he or she has a professional responsibility. Further, such relationships may have the effect of undermining the atmosphere of trust on which the educational process depends. Implicit in the idea of professionalism is the recognition by those in positions of authority that in their relationships with students there is always an element of power. It is incumbent upon those with authority not to abuse, nor to seem to abuse, the power with which they are entrusted.

> Officers and other members of the teaching staff should be aware that any romantic involvement with their students makes them liable for formal action against them if a complaint is initiated by a student. Even when both parties have consented to the development of such a relationship, it is the officer or instructor who, by virtue, of his or her special responsibility, will be held accountable for unprofessional behavior.

Dovan, et al. (1987) also reported that women's adherence to the organizational model promoted their empowerment. Women who espoused this explanatory model reported seeking redress for the victimization. Such a response would not be predicted from adherence to the sociocultural model: women would not be likely to take interpersonally assertive action or to act on an expectation that the organization will help them resolve the issue. Women are much more likely than men to assign a central role to the college for preventing and dealing with all levels of sexual harassment. Since the research indicates that men attribute more responsibility to women victims of sexual harassment, men would also be likely to minimize the potential responsibility of college/university officials (Paludi, 1990). As male faculty reported in the Fitzgerald et al. (1988:337) study:

> In a classroom setting it is entirely appropriate that personal and professional lives be separated. However, undergraduates doing honor's research and graduate students become junior colleagues; a close personal relationship is to be encouraged.
>
> It has been my observation that students, and some faculty, have little understanding of the extreme pressure a male professor can feel as the object of sexual interest of attractive women students.

Fitzgerald et al. reported that male faculty members typically do not label their behavior as sexual harassment despite the fact they report they frequently engage in initiating personal relationships with women students. Male faculty members denied the inherent power differential between faculty and students, as well as the psychological power conferred by this differential. Furthermore, Kenig and Ryan (1986) reported that faculty men were less likely than faculty women to define sexual harassment as including jokes, teasing remarks of a sexual nature and unwanted suggestive looks or gestures. In addition, women faculty were more likely than men to disapprove of romantic relationships between faculty and students. Male faculty typically view sexual harassment as a personal, not an organizational issue.

This data thus suggests that education is needed in men's perceptions of the misuse of power, their perceptions about women who have been harassed, and their attitudes toward sexual interactions. Another focus of such training lies in the politics involved in the mentor-protégé relationship. Typically, this relationship is not clearly conceptualized. Consequently, students and faculty do not share similar definitions of mentor and protégé (Haring-Hidore & Brooks, 1986; Paludi, 1987). Fitzgerald, Weitzman, Gold, and Ormerod (1988) reported that male faculty members who participated in their study typically denied that there exists an inherent power differential between students and faculty. Women students, however, recognize this power differential. Thus, educational programs are needed to deal with women's and men's understanding of the concept of harassment and the social meanings attributed to behaviors that legally constitute harassment. Truax (cited in Fitzgerald, 1986:24) claimed

> men's perceptions of what their behavior means are vastly different from women's. . . . We find, in working with victims of sexual harassment that there is often little disagreement with what has happened between student and professor, but rather, with what the conduct means. Professors will try to justify their behavior on the grounds that they are just friendly and trying to make a student feel welcome, or they thought that the student would be flattered by the attention.

However, the interpretation given to the professor's behavior by women students is not flattery or friendliness. The consequences of being harassed to undergraduate and graduate women have been devastating to their physical well-being, emotional health, and vocational development, including depression, insomnia, headaches, helplessness, decreased motivation (Whitmore, 1983). The behavior that legally constitute harassment is just that, despite what the professor's intentions may be. It is the power differential and/or the woman's reaction to the behavior that are the critical variables. As Zalk (1990) argued:

> The bottom line in the relationship between faculty member and student is POWER. The faculty member has it and the student does not. As intertwined as the faculty-student roles may be, and as much as one must exist for the other to exist, they are not equal collaborators. The student does not negotiate—indeed, has nothing to negotiate with.

Several kinds of intervention may be instituted in order to challenge attitudes that perpetuate harassment. As Biaggio, Brownell, and Watts (1990) suggest, key individuals within organizations can be targeted—residence hall advisors in dormitories, department chairs—for attendance at workshops at which they can be informed about the institutional policy and procedures dealing with harassment. In addition, new student orientations are another arena for disseminating information about institutional policies that prohibit sexual and gender harassment. Items relating to gender and sexual harassment can be placed on teaching evaluations.

Sandler (1988) has also offered suggestions for meeting this goal, including (1) establishing a policy statement that makes it clear that differential treatment of professional women on campus will not be tolerated, (2) establishing a permanent committee to explore and report on professional climate issues, and (3) publishing an annual report on progress in regard to women on campus.

At Hunter College we have been involved in several educational programs for students, faculty, administrators, and staff. For example, a four-part workshop on sexual harassment for faculty was co-sponsored by the Employees Assistance Program. The workshop objectives included learning how formal and informal power or authority in the university setting is perceived by workers, learning the politics involved in such nonverbal gestures as touch, body position, personal space, and learning the social meanings attributed to behaviors that legally constitute sexual harassment.

Yet education, however successful, is not sufficient in itself to prevent sexual harassment or offer remedies when it occurs. Because sexual harassment occurs in this context of institutional power, individuals who have been victimized are often, understandably, reluctant to use the ordinary channels in the college or university for resolving complaints. This is especially true because of the humiliating and disorienting impact of sexual harassment, where the victim may experience the sort of self-doubt, self-blame, and sense of degradation common to victims of rape, incest, and battering. It is important, therefore, that the means of hearing and resolving complaints of sexual harassment should be distinct from the regular departmental and administrative hierarchies. The Panel operating at Hunter College since 1982 has successfully met this requirement. The members are appointed by the President of Hunter College, and the Panel reports to both the President and the Vice-President for Student Affairs/Dean of Students, but it is independent of the administrative structures of the President's office and the office of Student Services.

The fact that the Panel at Hunter guarantees that all procedures will be confidential and further guarantees that the individual bringing the complaint will decide whether to make a formal complaint also encourages individuals to contact Panel members to discuss a problem. Unless people—faculty, staff, and students—feel that they will have these protections, they will seldom report the sexual harassment they have experienced. Research findings fully support this conclusion. Obviously, individual complaints cannot be resolved and the pervasive injury done to the college community by sexual harassment cannot be remedied unless complaints are actually reported.

In the six years' experiences of the Panel at Hunter College, most people make initial contact with the Panel for informal discussions about their discomfort in a situation that may have involved sexual harassment. Often they do not realize—because of general misunderstanding of the nature of sexual harassment and the lack of open discussion about it—exactly what constitutes sexual harassment and what their rights are under CUNY Board of Trustees' policies and Titles VII and IX. They need to talk with someone who is well-informed about the problem and trained to discuss it. Often, too, informal discussions with a Panal member enable the person to deal with the problem on his or her own or lead to an informal resolution through the assistance of members of the Panel.

To promote the effective and equitable resolution of problems involving sexual harassment, it seems necessary to have:

(1) an explicit policy adopted by the college or university in compliance with the provision of Titles VII and IX, such as the policy of CUNY's Board of Trustees, applicable to all units of the system. Such a policy allows the university and college to uphold and enforce its policies against sexual harassment within its own community (including such severe penalties as loss of pay or position or tenure) without requiring victimized individuals to undertake the laborious, protracted, and costly process of seeking redress from the courts under Titles VII and IX.

(2) one body of individuals, delegated by the responsible to the President of the college, who are specially educated about the nature of sexual harassment and trained to deal with both complaints and those accused of sexual harassment fairly, sensitively, and confidentially. The Panel at Hunter has prepared extensive educational materials for new Panel members and regularly engages in training sessions, attends conferences, consults with experts at other campuses, and so forth. The Panel now includes two counselors and three psychologists whose research specializations include the area of sexual harassment. Several members of the Panel have collaborated on a textbook on sexual harassment on college campuses, "Ivory Power," which was published by SUNY Press in 1990.

(3) a body composed of faculty, staff, and students so that the whole college community is represented. Under Hunter's policies, a person may contact any member of the Panel for initial, informal discussion. In order to make access to the Panel as easy and as comfortable as possible, the college community, in terms of sex, sexual orientation, academic programs, and ranks, racial and ethnic background. Research has indicated, and the Panel's experience

has confirmed, that many individuals feel more comfortable contacting someone they identify as a peer, so that the more diverse the composition of the Panel in terms of status, sex, race, and so forth, the more access the Panel provides the community it serves.

(4) common definitions of sexual harassment and common procedures for resolving conflicts applied equitably throughout the college, regardless of the status of the complainant or the person complained against. Without a common procedure, inequities can easily occur in the effort to protect individuals' rights under Titles VII and IX.

As Mead (1978) argued, we need a new taboo on campus that demands we make new norms, not rely on masculine-biased definitions of success, career development, and sexuality. We need an ethic of care—and the restructuring of academic institutions so that caring can become a central and active value (Stimpson 1988). Educational training will not be sufficient to reach this goal: the relative power of women in the college/university system that underlies sexual harassment will need to be changed. And that means massive changes in the present institutional structures that dominate our college and university system.

References

Adams, J. W., Kottke, J. L., & Padgitt, J. S. 1983 "Sexual harassment of university students." Journal of College Student Personnel 24:484–490.

Bailey, N., & Richards, M. 1985 "Tarnishing the ivory tower: Sexual harassment in graduate training programs in psychology." Paper presented at the American Psychological Association, Los Angeles, CA.

Bennett-Alexander, D. D. 1987 "The supreme court finally speaks on the issue of sexual harassment—what did it say?" Women's Rights Law Reporter 10:65–78.

Betz, N., & Fitzgerald, L. F. 1987 The career psychology of women. New York: Academic Press.

Biaggio, M. K., Brownell, A., & Watts, D. 1990 "Addressing sexual harassment: Strategies for prevention and change." in M. Paludi (ed.), Ivory Power. Albany: SUNY Press.

Bond, M. 1988 "Division 27 sexual harassment survey: Definition, impact, and environmental context." The Community Psychologist 21:7–10.

Dovan, J., Grossman, M., Kindermann, J., Matula, S., Paludi, M. A., & Scott, C. A. 1987 "College women's attitudes and attributions about sexual and gender harassment." Symposium presented at the Association for Women in Psychology, Bethesda, MD.

Dziech, B., & Weiner, L. 1984 The lecherous professor: Sexual harassment on campus. Boston: Beacon Press.

Fitzgerald, L. F. 1986 "The lecherous professor: A study in power relations." Paper presented at the American Psychological Association, Washington, DC.

Fitzgerald, L. F., Shullman, S., Bailey, N., Gold, Y., Ormerod, M., & Weitzman, L. 1988 "The incidence and dimensions of sexual harassment in academia and the workplace." Journal of Vocational Behavior 32:152–175.

Fitzgerald, L. F., Weitzman, L., Gold, Y., & Ormerod M. 1988 "Academic harassment: Sex and denial in scholarly garb." Psychology of Women Quarterly 12:329–340.

Haring-Hidore, M., & Brooks, L. 1986 "Learning from the problems mentors in academe have perceived in relationships with protégés." Paper presented at the American Educational Research Association, Washington, DC.

Kenig, S., & Ryan, J. 1986 "Sex differences in levels of tolerance and attribution of blame for sexual harassment on a university campus." Sex Roles 15:535–549.

Koss, M. P. (1990). Changed lives. In M. A. Paludi (Ed.) *Ivory Power: Sexual harassment on campus*. Albany: SUNY Press.

Lott, B., Reilly, M. E., & Howard, D. R. 1982 "Sexual assault and harassment: A campus community case study." Signs 8:296–319.

May, R. 1972 Power and innocence. New York: Dell.

Mead, M. 1978 "A proposal: We need new taboos on sex at work." Reported in B. Dzeich & L. Weiner (1984). The lecherous professor. Boston: Beacon Press.

Paludi, M. A. 1987 "Women and the mentor-protégé relationship: A feminist critique for the inadequacy of old solutions." Paper presented at the Interdisciplinary Congress on Women, Dublin, IR.

Paludi, M. A. (1990) Ivory power. Albany: SUNY Press.

Project on the Status and Education of Women 1978 Sexual harassment: A hidden issue. Washington, DC: Association of American Colleges.

Sandler, B. 1988 "Sexual harassment: A new issue for institutions, or these are the times that try men's souls." Paper presented at the Conference on Sexual Harassment on Campus, New York, NY.

Stimpson, C. 1988 "Overreaching: Sexual harassment and education." Paper presented at the Conference on Sexual Harassment, New York, NY.

Tangri, S., Burt, M., & Johnson, L. 1982 "Sexual harassment at work: Three explanatory models." Journal of Social Issues, 38:33–54.

Whitmore, R. 1983 Sexual harassment at UC Davies. Davis: Women's Resources and Research Center.

Wilson, K. R., & Krauss, L. A. 1983 "Sexual harassment in the university." Journal of College Student Personnel 24:219–24.

Zalk, S. R. (1990) "The lecherous professor: Psychological profiles of professors who harass their women students." In M. Paludi (ed.), Ivory Power. New York: SUNY Press.

O   APPENDIX **6**

The Incidence and Dimensions of Sexual Harassment in Academia and the Workplace

Louis Fitzgerald, Sandra Shullman, Nancy Bailey, Margaret Richards, Janice Swecker, Yael Gold, Mimi Ormerod, and Lauren Weitzman; reprinted here with permission from Academic Press.

Although only recently reaching public and scholarly awareness as an important issue, the sexual harassment of women workers has been a problem for as long as women have worked outside the home. Goodman (1981) notes that "the history of sexual harassment dates back at least to the time women first traded their labor in the marketplace" (p. 449). In 1908, a popular periodical of the day published a collection of stories documenting the experiences of women who had migrated to the city at the turn of the century to find work. These stories revealed widespread and extensive harassment. Bularzik (1978), in a historical account of the phenomenon, tells of a broom factory where women carried knives to protect themselves—contemporary accounts, while usually less dramatic, are no less compelling.

Although sexual harassment has been thought to have serious negative effects on women's career development, data regarding the prevalence of the phenomenon have, until recently, been scarce, and what data did exist could be criticized for the somewhat simplistic manner in which they were collected (e.g., Safran, 1976). Recently, however, two large-scale formal studies have appeared that lend support to the hypothesis that sexual harassment is indeed a widespread phenomenon. In 1980, the first comprehensive national survey of sexual harassment was initiated by the U.S. Merit Systems Protection Board. Data were collected from a stratified random sample of federal employees listed in the Central Personnel Data File of the Office of Personnel Management. Usable data were obtained from 83.8% of the 23,964 persons who received the questionnaire. The final sample contained 10,644 women. Forty-two percent of these women reported being the target the overt sexual harassment at some point in the 2-year period covered by the study. As Chapman (1981) points out, this is likely an underestimate, given the narrow definition of sexual harassment employed; even so, it projects to roughly 18 to 19 million employees in the total U.S. labor force in 1980. Similarly, in a large survey of a representative sample of private-sector workers in the Los Angeles area (Gutek, 1981), 53.1% of the women respondents reported experiencing at least one incident that they considered sexual harassment during their working lives.

Given that the phenomenon appears to be widespread, what can be said about its effects on women, and in what ways does it constitute a barrier to their career development? Farley (1978) cites a study conducted at the United Nations in which over 50% of the female respondents reported that they had personally experienced sexual pressure or knew other women who had experienced such pressure in situations involving promotion, recruitment, obtaining a permanent contract, transfer, and going on missions. Thirty-one percent of the women in Gutek's (1981) study had experienced some negative employment consequence, including being fired. Negative consequences in the Merit System study included emotional or physical difficulties, negative feelings about work, and poor job performance. Goodman (1981) writes:

> The picture of sexual harassment that emerges as understanding of the phenomenon grows is not only one of a common experience, but also a damaging one. Physical symptoms like headache, backache, nausea, weight loss or gain, and psychological reactions, like insomnia, depression, and nervousness, are common. A study by Working Women's Institute (Crull 1979) found sixty-three percent of the women who were sexually harassed suffered physical symptoms and ninety-six percent suffered symptoms of emotional stress. These reactions in turn cause loss of motivation, absenteeism, and, in the end, diminished productivity, as women lose their desire and ability to work efficiently. (p. 456)

Goodman goes on to cite evidence that plaintiffs in many of the early sexual harassment cases were fired from their jobs (*Tomkins v. PSE & G Co.*, 1977; *Williams v. Saxbe*, 1981; *Miller v. Bank of America*,

1979, et al.). It is difficult to escape the conclusion that sexual harassment constitutes one of the most ubiquitous and damaging barriers to women's career success and satisfaction.

Nor is sexual harassment limited to the workplace, although the harassment of women students by their professors has been called a "hidden issue" (Project on the Education and Status of Women, 1978). In their recent book on the topic, Dziech and Weiner (1984) write: "Sexual harassment of college students by their professors is a fact of campus life that many educators learn to ignore, and, in their silence, accept" (p. 1). Although it has only recently been recognized and named, such harassment is not a new problem, but one that women students have always faced. Writing for the Modern Language Association's Commission on the Status of Women, Franklin and her colleagues (Franklin, Moglen Zatling-Boring, & Angress, 1981) suggest:

> On occasion, in certain forms, it appeared as romance: the naive student swept into bed by her brilliant professor. . . . Charlotte Bronte wrote about it more than a hundred years ago; in the popular confessions magazines, authors write about it still. In functional form, it remains the stuff that fantasies are made of, fantasies that reflect and reinforce the tendency of our society to limit the definition of women to the sexual and domestic spheres and to soften . . . the linking of sexual dominance with the powerful and of sexual submission with the powerless. (p. 3)

In recent years, the growing interest in sexual harassment in the work-place and the accumulating body of case law have led to a parallel interest in defining and documenting the phenomenon in institutions of higher learning. As Crocker and Simon (1981) have noted, "Formal education is, in the United States, an important factor in an individual's career possibilities and personal development, therefore stunting or obstructing that person's educational accomplishment can have severe consequences" (p. 542). Thus, to the degree that sexual harassment exists in academic settings, it constitutes a serious external barrier to women's career development.

As with the research on working women, evidence exists that such harassment can result in serious psychological and practical consequences for women students. According to Dziech and Weiner (1984) such harassment often "forces a student to forfeit work, research, educational comfort, or even career. Professors withhold legitimate opportunities from those who resist, or students withdraw rather than pay certain prices" (p. 10). The practical costs of harassment to the victim are quite dramatic and have been documented by both survey and qualitative research efforts. For example, a 1983 study conducted at Harvard University and reported in the Chronicle of Higher Education indicated that 15% of the graduate and 12% of the undergraduate student victims in this survey changed their major or educational program as a result of the harassment; Adams, Kottke, & Padgitt (1983) report that 13% of the women students they surveyed said they had avoided taking a class or working with certain professors because of the risk of being subjected to sexual advances.

In the last few years, studies have begun to appear that attempt to document in a formal manner the nature and extent of sexual harassment in the university setting. Several institutions have undertaken self-studies, as well as attempted to determine what various constituencies (e.g., students and professors) believe constitutes sexual harassment. As a result of the differing methodologies and definitions that have been utilized, it has proven quite difficult to compare results across studies and to achieve some clarity concerning both the base rates and the dimensions of the phenomenon. In the most comprehensive treatment of the subject to date, Dziech and Weiner (1984) suggest that a figure of 30% appears to be a reliable estimate at present and call for the development of a standardized survey instrument that individual campuses could use to measure frequency so a national profile can be drawn.

This paper describes the results of research undertaken to provide such an instrument, which we call the Sexual Experiences Questionnaire (SEQ). The following sections will detail the instrument's development, results of psychometric analyses undertaken (including reliability and validity), and the results of the application of the inventory to two large public universities. In addition, we describe the development of a second form of the inventory designed for working women and report the results for a large sample of academic, professional and semiprofessional, and blue-collar women.

Study 1

Method

Sample

The sample for this initial study consisted of 2,599 students enrolled in either a Midwestern or a West Coast university. The universities were similar in size, both enrolling somewhat less than 20,000 students; however, they differed in prestige as well as location, with one being a highly prestigious research-oriented institution, housing many nationally known graduate programs. The sample at University 1 consisted of 903 women (N = 349 graduate women and 554 undergraduates) and 491 undergraduate men, enrolled in over 70 academic disciplines. The average age of the undergraduates was 22.78, whereas the graduate women averaged 32.29. Ninety-three percent of the undergraduates were advanced students and were approximately equally split between juniors and seniors.

The sample at University 2 consisted of 1,205 students (534 undergraduate women, 309 graduate women, and 362 undergraduate men). These students were similar to those at University 1, with the average age of the undergraduates being 22.26 and that of the graduate women 32.38. Almost 84% of the undergraduates had upper-class status, with juniors representing 32.21% of the total and seniors 51.70%.

Procedure

The procedure followed was similar at both institutions. First, a stratified random sample of upper-division classes was identified, and permission was sought from instructors to enter class and gather data. Classes in mathematics, engineering, and the so-called "hard sciences" were systematically oversampled to ensure adequate representation of women majoring in nontraditional areas. Participation was voluntary, and virtually all students participated and returned usable data (> 99%). At University 1, additional data were gathered from the Introductory Psychology pool. For this portion of the data collection, the study was given an innocuous title, and students signed up on the basis of schedule compatibility.

Finally, graduate women were contacted by mail and requested to participate. At University 1, an alphabetically stratified random sample of graduate women enrolled during the winter term of 1985 received research materials. These included the survey, along with a postage-paid, return envelope, and sealed debriefing materials. These were stamped with instructions indicating that they were to be opened only after the research packet had been completed and returned. Graduate women at University 2 were contacted in a similar manner during the winter term of 1986. The return rate for both parts of the graduate subsample was slightly over 40%, with no follow-up.

Instrument

The first step in instrument development was the generation of an initial item pool, based on the five levels of sexual harassment identified by Till (1980) through content analysis of his national survey of college women. Thus, items were identified from the literature or written by the project staff to measure five general areas:

1. *Gender harassment:* generalized sexist remarks and behavior;

2. *Seductive behavior:* inappropriate and offensive, but essentially sanction-free, sexual advances;

3. *Sexual bribery:* solicitation of sexual activity or other sex-linked behavior by promise of rewards;

4. *Sexual coercion:* coercion of sexual activity by threat of punishment;

5. *Sexual assault:* gross sexual imposition or assault.

All items were written in behavioral terms, and the words "sexual harassment" did not appear until the end of the questionnaire, thus avoiding the necessity for the respondent to make a subjective judgment as to whether or not she had been harassed before she could respond. It seems reasonable to suppose that individual differences exist in the perceptions and personal definitions of harassment, thus leading to possible confusion on the part of individuals as to whether or not they have "really been harassed." The present instrument attempted to avoid this problem by eliminating the subjectivity involved in making such a judgement.

Scoring. For each item, subjects were instructed to circle the response most closely describing their own experiences. The response options included: (1) Never, (2) Once, and (3) More than Once. If the subject circled (2) or (3), she was further instructed to indicate whether the person involved was a man or a woman (or both, if it happened more than once) by circling M, F, or B. The SEQ is designed primarily to identify the frequency of various types of harassment and thus is scored simply by counting the number of subjects who endorse the *Once* or *More than Once* response options for each item. (The distinction between *Once* and *More than Once* was introduced to control for the possible tendency of subject who had experienced a low-level or "nontraumatic" harassment behavior on a single occasion to dismiss that experience because "it only happened once." Although this proved useful in data *collection,* in practice it did not seem a worthwhile distinction for *scoring*. Thus, these two options were collapsed for scoring purposes.) In addition to item frequencies and percentages, it is possible to compute *level* frequencies and percentages by computing the number of subjects who endorse at least one item within a given area of harassment (gender harassment, seduction, etc.). Although it is theoretically possible to compute individual scores or profiles on the SEQ, the meaning of such scores is questionable until much more research has been carried out, not only on the SEQ itself, but also on its correlates. Thus, such a scoring procedure does not seem advisable at this time.

Pilot. Following initial construction of the inventory, it was piloted on a sample of 468 students at University 1, both graduate and undergraduate, male and female. Data were collected from intact classes in the College of Education whose instructors agreed to participate. Student participation was voluntary, and virtually all students agreed to cooperate. Classes included graduate classes in counseling, educational and school psychology, early childhood education, and special education, as well as undergraduate sections of various teacher education courses.

These students were asked to respond to the SEQ and to comment on the items, their clarity, relevance, and so forth. Based on this feedback, wording changes were made in several items, and two items that appeared open to varying interpretations were dropped. The original intent had been to design an inventory of 50 items (10 on each scale) plus the criterion item ("I have been sexually harassed"). However, in practice it proved difficult to construct this many items without considerable redundancy. In particular, Levels 3 and 4 (bribery and threat) appeared to be completely covered by four items each. Thus, the pilot version contained 30 items (7 each for Levels 1, 2, and 5; 4 items each for Levels 3 and 4; and the criterion item). On the basis of subject feedback, two items were dropped from Level 2, and the final form of the SEQ consisted of 28 items, of which 7 measured gender harassment (Level 1), 5 measured seductive behavior (Level 2), 4 each focused on sexual bribery and coercion (Levels 3 and 4, respectively), 7 designed to measure the general area of sexual assault, and the criterion item.

Reliability. Initial psychometric analysis, using Cronbach's coefficient α, yielded an internal consistency coefficient of .92 for the entire 28–item questionnaire on the University 1 sample ($N = 1395$); α computed on the University 2 sample was comparable. Test-retest stability on a small subsample of University 1 graduate students ($N = 46$) yielded a stability coefficient of .86 over a 2-week period.

Corrected split-half reliability coefficients for the five "scales" of the SEQ ranged from .62 to .86 and averaged .75. Comparable results were obtained for the University 2 sample.

Validity. Content validity was built into the SEQ through basing item construction on Till's (1980) empirically derived categories. In addition, the correlation of each item with the criterion item ("I have been sexually harassed") was examined. With the exception of two sexual bribery items that showed very little variance and one item measuring gender harassment, all items were significantly positively correlated with the criterion item. In addition, if the five areas of sexual harassment are considered as *levels* (following Till's formulation), the average item-criterion correlations for these five levels conformed, with one exception, to theoretical expectation, ranging from $r = .15$ for Level 1 (gender harassment) to $r = .37$ for Level 4 (sexual coercion). The coefficient for Level 5 (sexual assault) was lower than expected, most likely because several items showed very little variance. In general, it appeared that the SEQ possessed sufficient validity for research purposes.

Results

Frequencies and percentages are reported separately for University 1 and 2, for male and female students, and for graduate and undergraduate women. These results are then compared through the use of loglinear modeling procedures.

University 1

Four hundred forty-eight women, or approximately 50% of the sample, answered at least one of the items in the positive direction. (For purposes of the present discussion, no distinction is made between those women who report experiencing a situation once and those who report experiencing it more than once.) The items, and their percentage of endorsement, separately by institution and subsample, appear in Table 1.

As might be expected, the most frequently reported situations were those involving gender harassment or seduction. Of the 10 most frequently endorsed items, all were Level 1 or Level 2 situations. However, over 8% of the total sample reported having been subjected to unwanted stroking or fondling; approximately 8% had been directly propositioned; and nearly 5% of the total sample had been either subtly bribed or threatened with retaliation for refusing sexual advances. Despite the severity of many of these situations (e.g., touching, fondling, propositions, and threats) only 5% of the

Table 1

Percentage of Sample Endorsing Each Item on the SEQ by Educational Status, Gender, and University

SEQ Item	Undergraduate Women		Graduate Women		Undergraduate Men	
	Univ. 1 (N = 554)	Univ. 2 (N = 534)	Univ. 1 (N = 349)	Univ. 2 (N = 309)	Univ. 1 (N = 491)	Univ. 2 (N = 362)
Level 1: Gender Harassment:						
1.1 Suggestive stories or offensive jokes	42.30	34.46	38.00	44.66	36.30	25.52
1.2 Crudely sexual remarks	31.00	22.31	26.00	32.36	25.10	21.00
1.3 Seductive remarks	17.20	15.10	21.60	30.20	8.10	5.53
1.4 Staring, leering, ogling	27.02	20.42	23.63	33.12	10.50	5.63
1.5 Use of sexist or pornographic teaching materials	15.97	20.60	14.66	20.78	16.80	12.44
1.6 Treated "differently" due to gender	47.46	40.53	47.54	60.65	35.50	30.11
1.7 Sexist remarks about career options	37.75	29.13	36.02	49.02	26.00	21.82
Level 2: Seduction						
2.1 Unwanted discussion of personal or sexual matters	11.01	6.58	12.94	18.57	4.40	2.76
2.2 Unwelcome seductive behavior (requests for dates, drinks, back-rubs, etc.)	19.68	15.25	20.40	29.77	7.40	3.49
2.3 Unwanted sexual attention	14.62	10.96	19.60	27.04	3.20	<2.00
2.4 Attempts to establish a romantic sexual relationship	8.30	7.74	12.36	21.68	2.90	<2.00
2.5 Propositions	7.64	4.73	8.36	13.68	3.20	<2.00

Table 1—*Continued*

SEQ Item	Undergraduate Women		Graduate Women		Undergraduate Men	
	Univ. 1 (N = 554)	Univ. 2 (N = 534)	Univ. 1 (N = 349)	Univ. 2 (N = 309)	Univ. 1 (N = 491)	Univ. 2 (N = 362)
Level 3: Sexual Bribery						
3.1 Subtle bribery for sexual cooperation	4.87	3.40	3.74	8.12	<2.00	<2.00
3.2 Direct offers of reward	<1.00	<1.00	<1.00	1.65	<1.00	<1.00
3.3 Engaged in unwanted sexual behavior due to promises of reward	<1.00	0	<1.00	<1.00	<1.00	0
3.4 Actually rewarded for sexual cooperation	<1.00	2.00	<1.00	3.25	2.20	2.21
Level 4: Sexual Coercion						
4.1 Subtle threats of retaliation for noncooperation	5.05	2.19	3.73	8.09	<2.00	<2.00
4.2 Direct threats	<1.00	<2.00	<1.00	<1.00	0	0
4.3 Engaged in unwanted sexual behavior due to threats of retaliation	<1.00	<1.00	<1.00	<2.00	<1.00	<1.00
4.4 Actually experienced negative consequences for sexual noncooperation	<1.00	<2.00	<1.00	7.77	<1.00	0

Table 1—Continued

SEQ Item	Undergraduate Women		Graduate Women		Undergraduate Men	
	Univ. 1 (N = 554)	Univ. 2 (N = 534)	Univ. 1 (N = 349)	Univ. 2 (N = 309)	Univ. 1 (N = 491)	Univ. 2 (N = 362)
Level 5: Sexual Imposition						
5.1 Unwanted attempts to touch or fondle	8.00	5.00	8.60	14.01	2.70	<2.00
5.2 Forceful attempts to touch or fondle	2.50	2.00	3.70	4.21	<1.00	0
5.4 A situation where a professor made unwanted attempts to have sex that resulted in the respondent crying, pleading, or physically struggling	0	<1.00	0	<2.00	0	0
5.7 Percentage of students reporting that they had been sexually harassed by a professor or instructor	3.80	4.14	7.49	15.85	1.50	0

Note: All items from the inventory are not listed here, as four items, each describing situations of extreme physical harassment, received almost no endorsement from the sample. Items are listed in considerably abbreviated form. Note that a zero indicates any figure smaller than one-half of 1% (e.g., .005).

total female sample indicated that they believed they had been sexually harassed. On a separate part of the questionnaire, 5% indicated that they had dropped a course to avoid such situations, while 15% and 21% of the undergraduate and graduate women, respectively, noted that they had avoided taking a course for this reason.

Only 3% had attempted to report a harassing situation; others indicated in general that (1) they felt they would not be believed; (2) they had not wanted to cause trouble and/or be labeled as troublemakers; or (3) they had either dealt with the situation themselves or had not felt it was serious enough to report.

The results for the male students are similar in that the most common behaviors reported were all Level 1 and Level 2 situations. As Table 1 details, the most frequently endorsed items had to do with situations where professors or instructors habitually told suggestive stories or offensive jokes (36.3%); situations where the student was treated "differently" because he was male (35.5%); situations where the professor or instructor made sexist remarks (26%); or situations where a professor made crudely sexual remarks (25.1%). With the exception of an item concerning sexist of pornographic teaching materials (16.8%), no other situations had been experienced by more than 10% of the male sample, and most items received much lower frequencies of endorsement (mean percentage of endorsement = 2.47).

University 2

Six hundred thirty-one women, or approximately 76%, answered at least one of the items in the affirmative direction. Again, no distinction is made here between those women who indicated experiencing a situation once as opposed to more than once. The percentages of endorsement for this sample are also displayed in Table 1, presented in the order in which they appear on the inventory.

As with University 1, the most frequently reported situations were those involving gender harassment or seduction. Of the 10 most frequently endorsed items, all were Level 1 or Level 2. For the undergraduates, no behavior classified as Level 3, 4, or 5 was experienced by more than 5% of the sample, although exactly 5% reported unwanted attempts by a professor to touch or fondle them, 4.73% reported being propositioned, and 3.4% reported being subtly bribed with some sort of reward (e.g., grades and preferential treatment) to engage in sexual activity. Slightly over 4% (4.14%) believed that they had been sexually harassed.

Among the graduate women, nearly 30% reported receiving unwelcome seductive behavior from their professors; 14% reported unwanted attempts to touch or fondle them; over 8% felt that they had been subtly bribed (the same percentage who felt they had been subtly threatened) to engage in sexual activity with a professor; nearly 8% had actually experienced negative consequences for not being sexually cooperative; and over 4% had been subjected to forceful attempts to touch, kiss, or grab them. Nearly 16% reported that they believed they had been sexually harassed.

The percentages of endorsement for the male students at University 2 also appear in Table 1. As this table reveals, only Level 1 items (gender harassment) achieved an endorsement rate of greater than 3.5%. The modal endorsement rate was 1% or less. Only one out of the 362 subjects indicated that he believed he had been sexually harassed (by a male faculty member).

Comparisons among the Samples

The item responses of the female subjects at the two universities were examined through loglinear modeling procedures to explore the possibility of group differences attributable to the effect of university setting or student status (graduate or undergraduate). Conceptually similar to factorial analysis of variance in producing main effects and interactions, loglinear modeling is a procedure for analyzing multiway contingency tables to determine the relationships among multiple categorical variables. Responses to 19 of the 28 SEQ items were modeled (9 items, all dealing with severe forms of harassment such as sexual coercion and imposition, had levels of endorsement that were too low to analyze reliably). Of these 19, 16 yielded a significant three-way interaction, indicating that the pattern of experiences were different for the graduate and undergraduate women at the two universities. When the resulting contingency tables were examined, it was found that, in every case, the undergraduate women at University 1 and the graduate women at University 2 reported more harassment than their respective same-university colleagues. Although three of these comparisons demonstrated probability levels somewhat below the .003 required to hold the overall significance level at .05 for 19 comparisons using Bonferonni's procedure, the complete consistency of the pattern of response allows considerable confidence that the findings on these three "weak" items were not due to chance.

Three items did not manifest the three-way interaction. Analysis of these items indicated that in two cases, the item responses could be modeled without the interaction terms corresponding to University or Student Status X Response, indicating that these variables were not associated with differential responses.

The third case was the criterion item, "I have been sexually harassed." The University I sample demonstrated statistically significant differences between the graduate and undergraduate women (likelihood ratio $\chi^2 = 5.64$, $\rho < .02$). As a descriptive measure of the strength of association, odds ratios (Reynolds, 1977) were computed and indicated that, at University 1, the odds were twice as great that a graduate woman would perceive herself as having been harassed as compared to an undergraduate woman. When the University 2 sample was examined, the results were similar, but stronger (likelihood ratio $\chi^2 = 33.35$, $\rho < .001$); among these women, the odds were nearly 4.5 as great that a graduate student would report that she had been sexually harassed.

Finally, the experiences of the male and female undergraduates were compared, using simple χ^2 procedures. For the students at University 1, 20 items had sufficient variance in both the male and female samples to analyze reliably. On 15 items, the women showed significantly higher levels of endorsement, and 10 of these demonstrated probabilities at or below the .003 required for an overall significance level of .05. Of the 5 items on which there were no gender differences, 3 tapped extremely unusual experiences (such as direct threats, rewards actually received for sexual cooperation, and so forth). The other 2 items that the men and women endorsed equally had to do with (1) crudely sexual remarks, either public or private; and (2) the use of sexist or suggestive teaching materials.

In the University 2 sample, 19 items yielded enough variance to examine reliably. Fourteen of these showed significant gender differences, all but 2 of these beyond the .003 level. In every case, the women were significantly more likely to endorse the item than were the men. Five items showed no differences. As with University 1, 4 of these described unusual experiences; the fifth was one of the Level 1 items that had previously demonstrated no gender differences at University 1.

Study 2

Long before sexual harassment was identified as a problem for women students in higher education, it had been identified as an external barrier to the vocational adjustment of women in the world of work. As we noted above, what evidence existed strongly suggested that such behavior was both widespread and debilitating to women workers (Betz & Fitzgerald, 1987). However, data gathering was largely nonsystematic, plagued by the lack of a theoretical base and the absence of a widely accepted definition of the phenomenon, as well as any standardized measuring instrument—all issues the SEQ was designed to address. Thus, it seemed reasonable to attempt an adaptation of this measure to address the issues of women already active in the world of work.

Method

Sample

The population of interest for this study was female faculty members, administrators, and staff employed at University 1 during the winter term of 1985 ($N = 642$). Thus, the population included both academic, professional, clerical, and blue-collar women. Research materials were sent to these women through campus mail, with a cover letter and sealed debriefing materials, similar to those received by the female graduate students. Usable replies were received from 307 women (a return rate of 48% with no follow-up). Of this number, about 20% were faculty, 20% were administrators, and 55% were staff, while 5% identified themselves as some combination of these categories or as being some other type of employee. The subjects were overwhelmingly Caucasian (94%) with a mean age of 38.05 and a median age of 39.

Instrument

Using the original form of the questionnaire as a point of departure, two focus groups were conducted by the project staff. Each of these groups was attended by 8–10 faculty and staff women. The items and levels of the SEQ were discussed with respect to their relevancy for employed women, and group members brainstormed to identify situations that were not adequately reflected by the items of the SEQ. As a result of these discussion groups, item wording was appropriately modified, and five new items were added (four to Level 2 and one to Level 5). The Level 2 items had to do with invasion of privacy and the spread of sexual insinuations and rumors, while the Level 5 item asked: "Have you ever been in a situation where a male co-worker deliberately touched you (e.g., laid a hand on your bare arm, or put an arm around your shoulders) in a way that made you feel uncomfortable?"

Instructions were modified to elicit information concerning experiences with male co-workers, and other men in the work environment, past or present. Response options were similar to those of the original SEQ; that is, the subjects were instructed to circle

(1) Never; (2) Once; or (3) More than Once. Since virtually none of our female student subjects reported harassment by women, and little or none has been reported in the literature, we asked this sample only about male co-workers. Reliability analysis, using Cronbach's α, indicated that the SEQ2 possesses satisfactory internal consistency α = .86).

Results

The frequency of endorsement for the items of the SEQ2 appears in Table 2, separately for each of the three types of women workers sampled (faculty, staff, and administrators). Differences among these three groups were then examined through simple contingency analysis. Finally, the experiences of the working women and the women students were compared through a similar procedure.

As table 2 details, these working women were most likely to report behaviors classified as gender harassment (Level 1), followed by seductive behavior (Level 2). Almost 6% reported that they had been subtly bribed to engage in sexual behavior with a co-worker, while slightly over 3% indicated that they had been subtly threatened with retaliation for noncooperation. With respect to Level 5 (gross sexual imposition or assault), over 11% reported that they had been subjected to unwanted attempts to stroke or fondle them, while one of the new items ["Have you ever been in a situation where a male co-worker deliberately touched you, (e.g., laid a hand on your bare arm, or put an arm around your shoulders) in a way that made you feel uncomfortable?"] elicited the highest rate of endorsement in the entire SEQ2 (50.82%). Slightly over 10% of the total sample reported that they believed they had been sexually harassed.

The subjects' responses were then compared based on the occupational group to which they belonged [faculty, staff (both white and blue collar) or administrator]. Twenty comparisons were made, including all of the Level 1 and 2 items and four of the Level 5 items. The frequencies for sexual coercion and the more severe forms of sexual imposition were too small to analyze reliably. Of the 20 comparisons, 9 produced a significant χ^2 statistic ($p < .05$), and 6 of these reached the .003 level of significance required to hold the overall significance level at .05 for the group of 20 comparisons. Examination of the associated contingency tables revealed that, in every case, the women administrators reported more experiences of harassment than either the faculty women or the staff. Despite this dif-

Table 2
Percentage of Working Women Endorsing Each Item on the SEQ by Type of Employee

	Faculty (N = 61)	Staff (N = 170)	Administrators (N = 61)	Total[a] (N = 306)
Level 1: Gender harassment				
1.1 Suggestive stories or offensive jokes	36.06	41.77	57.38	44.30
1.2 Crudely sexual remarks	22.95	25.29	39.34	26.39
1.3 Seductive remarks	26.23	29.41	44.26	31.27
1.4 Staring, leering, ogling	16.39	27.06	26.23	24.10
1.5 Display, use, or distribution of sexist material or pornography	13.12	24.12	29.51	21.82
1.6 Treated "differently" due to gender	62.30	40.59	75.41	50.82
1.7 Sexist remarks about women's behavior and career options	47.54	34.12	67.21	43.00
Level 2: Seduction				
2.1 Unwanted discussion of personal or sexual matters	21.31	17.06	26.23	19.22
2.2 Unwelcome seductive behavior	19.67	20.59	24.59	20.20
2.3 Unwanted sexual attention	18.03	17.06	24.59	18.24
2.4 Attempts to establish a sexual relationship, despite discouragement	6.56	11.18	19.67	11.40
2.5 Propositions	11.48	12.35	27.87	14.98
2.6 Invasion of privacy (repeated calling, requests for dates, "dropping in")	4.91	8.24	18.03	9.12
2.7 Sexual insinuations or innuendos	16.39	14.12	32.79	17.92
2.8 Crude or offensive sexual remarks made about the respondent to others	13.12	7.06	22.95	11.40
2.9 Sexual rumors spread about the respondent	8.20	4.12	26.23	9.12

Table 2—Continued

	Faculty (N = 61)	Staff (N = 170)	Administrators (N = 61)	Total[a] (N = 306)
Level 3: Bribery				
3.1 Subtle bribery for sexual cooperation	3.28	4.71	13.12	5.86
3.2 Direct bribery	3.28	2.94	1.64	2.60
3.4 Actually rewarded for sexual cooperation	0	<2.00	6.56	1.96
Level 4: Threat				
4.1 Subtle threats of retaliation for noncooperation	3.28	<2.00	9.84	3.25
4.2 Direct threats	0	0	<2.00	<1.00
4.3 Engaged in unwanted sexual behavior due to threats of retaliation	0	<2.00	<2.00	<1.00
4.4 Actually experienced negative consequences for sexual noncooperation	<2.00	<2.00	8.20	2.28
Level 5: Sexual Imposition				
5.1 Deliberate touching	49.18	38.82	60.66	50.82
5.2 Unwanted attempts to touch or fondle	6.56	12.94	14.75	11.40
5.3 Forceful attempts to touch or fondle	6.56	2.94	8.20	4.56
5.6 Attempts at intercourse that resulted in the respondent crying, pleading, or physically struggling	<2.00	0	<2.00	0
5.8 Have been sexually harassed	8.20	8.82	18.03	10.10

[a]This total includes 14 women who identified themselves as "Other" with respect to employment status. N = 306, as one subject did not reprt her employment category.

ferential pattern of experience, there were no group differences on the criterion item, "I have been sexually harassed."

Following this analysis, the student data were collapsed across university and student status and the data from the working women were similarly combined, and comparisons were performed to develop some beginning understanding of the relative experiences of the two groups. Of the 28 items common to the two forms of the SEQ, 21 had sufficient frequency of endorsement to permit reliable analysis; 7 of these comparisons produced a statistically significant χ^2, four of which reached the .003 level required to maintain overall α at .05. In each case, it was the working women who were significantly more likely to endorse the item. These significant items represented all five levels of the SEQ and included the criterion item, "I have been sexually harassed."

Discussion

The program of research described above was designed to investigate the dimensions and extend of sexual harassment in higher education and the workplace. This discussion begins by examining the properties of the SEQ and the more general question of the structure and nature of sexual harassment. Following this, a discussion of the type and extent of harassment is presented. Finally, the perceptions and labeling of harassment by women victims are explored, and the issue of gender differences in harassment is examined. Limitations of the research and future directions of investigation are also addressed.

Properties and Structure of the SEQ

Although a complete psychometric analysis of the SEQ is not possible here, an examination of the available data suggests that both forms possess sufficient reliability and stability for research use at this time. In addition to basic research, the SEQ appears promising as a measure of institutional needs assessment, as indicated by its ability to discriminate among the patterns of harassment experienced by women at different institutions and of differing educational statuses. Since it has been suggested that women in certain academic disciplines and occupational areas experience differing levels and types of harassment (e.g., Till, 1980), an examination of SEQ patterns of such groups might also prove promising (for example, women in traditional versus nontraditional occupational areas, or women students in the sciences as opposed to women in education, nursing, or other, more traditionally female, disciplines).

Criterion-related validity, as indexed by the correlation of the item, "I have been sexually harassed," with mean item endorsements of the proposed levels of harassment, is also promising, although complicated by the low levels of endorsement of the more severe items. In this respect, it should also be pointed out that factor analyses of the SEQ and SEQ2 (Fitzgerald & Shullman, 1985) fail to confirm the five-level structure proposed by Till (1980). Rather, a three-factor solution, in which bribery and threat collapse into one factor, seduction and sexual imposition group together as another, and gender harassment stands alone as a separate factor, appeared to more accurately account for the data. This structure was further supported through a complete-link cluster analysis of the University 1 data conducted by the first author (Fitzgerald, 1986), which yielded three clusters conforming to the original three factors.[1]

However, as with the criterion-related validity coefficients, all of these solutions must be considered tentative at this point, due to the unstable nature of the correlations computed on the items showing very little variance. These items, all dealing with relatively dramatic and extreme forms of behavior, yield extremely low levels of endorsement in all three samples, suggesting that frequency data, subject as it is to the vagaries of individual experience, may be unable to reliably support any form of structural analysis. Rather, a more appropriate data base could be developed by having subjects rate the items of the SEQ on some characteristic (e.g., severity, degree of psychological coercion, or even whether or not the behavior constituted sexual harassment). Alternatively, subjects could conduct a free-sort of the items. Such data could then be used to construct a proximity matrix, each of whose cells would be based on data from all the subjects. Such a matrix would provide a more suitable basis for examining the nature of the construct. Until this is done, it is not possible to either support or reject the hypothesized five-level structure.

The problems associated with the measurement of low-probability events are not, however, limited to the analysis of structure. Such items also demonstrate low item-total correlations and depressed scale-total correlations, as well as item/scale-criterion correlations. Thus, some of these items (for example, those tapping

---

[1] Copies of the interitem correlation matrix, as well as the instruments, are available from Fitzgerald on request.

experiences of rape and attempted rape) could probably be dropped from the inventory with little, if any, loss of information, while at the same time yielding substantial improvement in the psychometric qualities of the instrument. In this regard, it should be noted that, in our experience, subjects who do endorse these items almost invariably describe their experiences at length in the space provided for comments. Thus, data associated with these low-probability events will most likely by volunteered spontaneously by respondents.

In addition to such deletions, it seems reasonable that at least some of the items added to the working women's form of the SEQ (SEQ2) may work equally well for student populations and could thus profitably be added to the student form. Such revisions are currently being undertaken.

Type and Extent of Harassment Experienced

The first conclusion drawn from the present data sets is that gender harassment and seductive behaviors are the most common situations experienced by women students and workers . . . and they are experienced quite widely. On the average, slightly over 31% of women students and 34% of working women reported some form of gender harassment, while about 15% of the students and 17% of the employed women had experienced seductive sexual approaches from their professors or co-workers. These numbers can probably be considered a conservative estimate as incidence rates in some groups are considerably higher (the graduate women at University 2, for example). Such behaviors constitute what can be called *condition of work* (or education) harassment, and while not as widely recognized as the more dramatic quid pro quo behaviors discussed below, create an offensive and often intimidating environment in which women must work or study.

Direct sexual coercion, on the other hand, whether bribery or intimidation, appears much less widespread. No more than about 13% of any of the sample subgroups reported positive endorsement of any of the sexual intimidation items, and the average was considerably lower. In general, then, the classic form of quid pro quo sexual harassment was not as common as has sometimes been assumed (Dziech & Weiner, 1983), at least in the present samples. It seems reasonable to point out, however, that even 3% to 5% of these samples generalizes to hundreds of thousands of college women in this country, and several million working women. As Chapman (1981) has pointed out, some of the percentages may appear small, but the absolute numbers are not. In a similar fashion, while direct sexual assault is infrequent (although not unknown) sexual imposition is perhaps more frequent than might be expected. Between 5% and 14% of these women (depending on the subgroup to which they belonged) reported that they had experienced unwanted attempts to touch or fondle them, with approximately half of this number indicating that these attempts had been forceful in nature. In the sample of employed women, over half (50.82%) reported that they had been deliberately touched or stroked by their male co-workers in a manner that made them uncomfortable. While not all touching is sexual, of course, or necessarily inappropriate, this figure does give some sense of the extent of the phenomenon.

Perceptions and Labeling of Harassment

One of the more puzzling aspects of sexual harassment is the finding that large numbers of women who have experienced relatively blatant instances of such behavior fail to recognize and label their experiences as such. It was because of this possibility that the decision was made to write the items of the SEQ completely in behavioral terms and to eliminate all references to "sexual harassment" except for the criterion item. The usefulness of this strategy was borne out by the data from the present samples. Despite the widespread nature of some of the behaviors reported here (for example, nearly 28% of the women administrators reported that they had been propositioned by male co-workers, while 27% of the graduate women at University 2 noted that they had received unwelcome attention from a professor or instructor) relatively few women reported that they believed they had been sexually harassed. Overall, only about 5% of the women at University 1, 10% of the women at University 2, and 10% of the employed women answered this item affirmatively.

These group figures, however, obscure some interesting differences in perceptions. For example, in both university samples, the odds were much greater that a graduate woman would perceive herself as harassed; this was true despite the fact that actual experience of harassment was not directly related to student status, but rather was an interactive function of status and environment (i.e., university setting).

The working women, on the other hand, did not differ among themselves in their frequency of response, but were significantly more likely than the combined student sample to perceive that they had been harassed. And their experiences bore them out, at least to some degree.

These data combine to suggest that the perception and labeling of one's experiences as constituting sexual harassment may be a function of (at least) two variables; the actual extent and severity of those experiences and age. It will be recalled that the graduate women were approximately 10 years older than the undergraduate women, while the working women were almost 10 years older still. The graduate and undergraduate women did not differ directly in their experiences of harassment, although they labeled them differently, while the working women were more likely than the students to report experiences *as well as* perceptions that were harassing in nature.

Future research should examine these issues more closely, as well as investigating other possible explanatory variables (e.g., attitudes toward women and the like). Although such experiences can no doubt lead to conflict or frustration whether or not they are labeled as harassment, such labeling likely mediates psychological reactions (in either a positive or a negative way) as well as influencing the choice of coping mechanism. An additional point in this regard is that made by Betz and Fitzgerald (1987) who observe:

> (Some) studies seem to imply that if a behavior is not *perceived* as harassment, then it is not. Such interpretations are clearly incorrect. Sexual harassment is well defined in legal terms, and the behaviors defined as harassment are just that, whatever one's "perceptions" may be. Research in this area should take care to point this out, lest important and theoretically meaningful data on individual differences in perceptions be misconstrued to dismiss or trivialize this extremely important barrier to women's career adjustment (p. 245).

Gender Differences

Another conclusion, based on the two university data sets, is that men (at least male students) are quite unlikely to be harassed. Although sexual harassment is generally perceived as a barrier to *women's* career development (Fitzgerald & Betz, 1983; Betz & Fitzgerald, 1987; Nieva & Gutek, 1981), some have suggested that it may also be a problem for men. Our findings, like those of other investigators, suggest that this is unlikely to be so. Both Kottke (1981) and Metha and Nigg (1983) report that only 5% of male respondents at their universities reported being sexually harassed. In a study more similar to the present one, but with a smaller sample ($N = 173$ male students), Reilly, Lott, and Gallogly (1986) found the percentages of men reporting harassing behaviors to be quite low. For example, anywhere from 1.2% to 7.7% of the male students reported experiencing harassing behaviors on the part of women professors. Even these figures represent a somewhat inflated picture, as no item was endorsed by more than 2% of the sample except the somewhat ambiguous one of "sexually suggestive looks" (7.7%). Similarly, in the present sample, harassing experiences other than Level 1 (gender harassment) were virtually nonexistent. And, it is unclear the extent to which male students experience these situations (i.e., suggestive stories or jokes and being treated differently because of gender) as inappropriate or unpleasant, much less harassing. Indeed, although our data do not allow us to answer this question, it is possible, or even likely, that many of these Level 1 items reflect a *favoring* of male students, rather than otherwise. While it is clear that sexual behavior in the classroom or workplace is inappropriate no matter the target, it is equally clear that this is overwhelmingly a barrier for *women* students and workers; it seems reasonable to conclude that future studies in this area are unlikely to yield either new data or different insights.

Limitations and Future Directions

The research program described above suffers from the usual limitations on generalizability, although possibly less so than with the more typical one-sample study. In particular, however, we are quite limited in drawing conclusions concerning employed women. Although we covered at least three occupational groups (one of which, the staff group, was quite heterogeneous), the subjects all worked in the same institution. And that institution was a university, a setting that can be expected to differ in systematic, although at this point unknown, ways from other organizational contexts. Those of us who live and work in academia would probably like to point out that incidences of harassment reported in the working women sample, while notable, are markedly lower than those reported in studies of the nonacademic workplace. Until our research is extended, however, we must more parsimoniously attribute these results to differing methodologies between our work and those of other researchers.

With respect to our student samples, we obviously are limited to statements concerning public universities. Whether patterns of behavior are different in community colleges, junior colleges, or elite private institutions is a matter of speculation at this point. If the SEQ fulfills its promise as reasonable instrumentation, it would seem important to draw the national profile discussed by

Dziech and Weiner (1984). Other interesting questions remain concerning possible differences among various educational and occupational groups, ethnic groups (a question we could not address with our largely Caucasian sample), the differing experiences of white and blue collar women, and so forth. Group differences in perceptions of harassment, discussed above with respect to structural considerations, may also yield interesting data upon which to construct theory.

Concluding Remarks

In summary, the central concept of sexual harassment is the misuse of power, whether organizationally or institutionally, in a manner that constructs a barrier to women's educational and occupational pursuits. As a thwarting condition that generates both frustration and conflict, and interferes with the woman's pursuit of her career goals, it satisfies the parameters of Crites's (1976) model of vocational adjustment. Although future research designed to identify coping mechanisms is both important and necessary, it seems reasonable to suggest that the only integrative solution is institutional and organizational change.

References

Adams, J. W., Kottke, J. L., & Padgitt, J. S. (1983). Sexual harassment of university students. *Journal of College Student Personnel, 24*, 484–90.

Backhouse, C., & Cohen, L. (1981). *Sexual harassment on the job.* New Jersey: Prentice-Hall.

Betz, N. E., & Fitzgerald, L. F. (1987). *The career psychology of women.* New York: Academic Press.

Bularzik, M. (1978). Sexual harassment at the workplace: Historical notes. *Radical America, 12*, 25–43.

Chapman, G. R. (Ed.) (1981). *Harassment and discrimination of women in employment.* ERIC Document No. ED 225054.

Crites, J. O. (1976). A comprehensive model of vocational development in early adulthood. *Journal of Vocational Behavior, 9*, 105–18.

Crocker, P. L., & Simon, A. E. (1981). Sexual harassment in education. *Capitol University Law Review, 10*, 541–84.

Crull, P. (1979). *The impact of sexual harassment on the job: A profile of the experiences of 92 women.* Working Women's Research Series, Report No. 3.

Dziech, B., & Weiner, L. (1984). *The lecherous professor*. Boston: Beacon Press.

Farley, L. (1978). *Sexual shakedown: The sexual harassment of women on the job*. New York: McGraw-Hill.

Fitzgerald, L. F. (1986). The structure of harassment. Unpublished manuscript, University of California, Santa Barbara.

Fitzgerald, L. F., & Betz, N. E. (1983). Issues in the vocational psychology of women. In W. B. Walsh and S. H. Osipow (Eds.), *Handbook of vocational psychology* (Vol. 1). Hillsdale, N.J.: Erlbaum.

Fitzgerald, L. F., & Shullman, S. L. (1985). The development and validation of an objectively scored measure of sexual harassment. Paper presented to the convention of the American Psychological Association, Los Angeles.

Franklin, P., Moglin, H., Zatling-Boring, P., & Angress, R. (1981). *Sexual and gender harassment in the academy*. New York: Modern Language Association.

Gutek, B. A. (1981). Experiences of sexual harassment: Results from a representative survey. Paper presented at the 89th Annual Convention of the American Psychological Association, Los Angeles, August.

Kottke, J. L. (1981). Conditions of and students attitudes toward sexual harassment. Paper presented at the Iowa/Midwest Regional Women's Studies Association Conference.

Livingston, J. (1982). Responses to sexual harassment on the job: Legal, organizational, and individual actions. *Journal of Social Issues, 38*, 5–22.

Meek, P., & Lynch, A. (1983). Establishing an informal grievance procedure for cases of sexual harassment of students. *Journal of the National Association for Women Deans and Counselors.*

Metha, A., & Nigg, J. (1983). Sexual harassment on campus: An institutional response. *Journal of the National Association of Women Deans and Counselors, 46*, 9–15.

Miller v. Bank of America, 418 F. Supp. 233 (N.D. Cal. 1976) revised, 600 F. 2d 211 (9th Circuit 1979).

Nieva, V. F., & Gutek, B. A. (1981). *Women and work: A psychological perspective*. New York: Praeger.

Project on the Status and Education of Women. (1978). *Sexual harassment: A hidden issue*. Washington, D.C.: Association of American Colleges.

Reilly, M. L., Lott, B., & Gallogly, S. M. (1986). *Sexual harassment of university students*. Paper presented to the convention of the Association for Women in Psychology, Oakland, Calif.

Reynolds, H. T. (1977). *The analysis of cross-classifications*. New York: Free Press.

Safran, C. (1976, March). What men do to women on the job. *Redbook*, pp. 45–51.

Tangri, S., Burt, M., & Johnson, L. (1982). Sexual harassment at work: Three explanatory models. *Journal of Social Issues, 38*, 33–54.

Till, F. (1980). *Sexual harassment: A report on the sexual harassment of students*. Washington, D.C.: National Advisory Council on Women's Educational Programs.

Tomkins v. Public Service Electric & Gas Co., 568 F. 2nd 1044 (3rd Circuit 1977).

Williams v. Saxbe, 12 FEP cases 1093 (1981).

Division 27 Sexual Harassment Survey: Definitions, Impact, and Environmental Context

By Meg Bond. Reprinted with permission from the Community Psychologist.

Research on women's professional development has identified sexual harassment in academic settings as a significant barrier. Previous research has clearly documented the existence of the problem on campuses throughout the United States. However, past research has not provided a consistently clear definition of sexual harassment and has rarely looked beyond prevalence estimates, attitudes toward harassment or sociological analyses that emphasize the role of power differences. There is a clear need to build on previous work to develop a more ecological approach to the problem that incorporates both individual and sociological perspectives. There is a need to explore an operational definition of sexual harassment that considers impact as well as behavioral occurrence. We also need to develop an understanding of the broader impact of sexual harassment on graduate training environments, and reciprocally, of the environmental components that support or inhibit sexual harassment. In this article, I will describe a survey on sexual harassment that begins to address the three issues of definition, impact and environment context.

The Committee on Women in Community Psychology conducted a survey of women in Division 27 during the Spring of 1986 (Bond & Linney, 1986). A number of general barriers to women's professional development were identified, primarily in areas related to supports in the immediate environment, both collegial kinds of support and technical supports. While the existence of these barriers clearly raises concerns, the most striking finding was that about

25% of the respondents reported being sexually harassed during their graduate training.

In depth exploration of the problem of sexual harassment was not one of the original survey goals, and thus, the results raised as many questions as they answered. First, it was unclear exactly what types of experiences women were experiencing as sexual harassment. Their comments indicated that they were referring to behaviors that ranged from sexist remarks to "sexual blackmail." Secondly, simply pointing out the existence of the problem provided little specific guidance for intervention or prevention efforts. We needed more information about the context of women's sexual harassment experiences. Consequently, I conducted a second survey in the Spring of 1987 guided by three focal questions: What are women's experiences of sexual harassment? What impact do these experiences have on women's professional development? and What qualities of the graduate school environment promote sexual harassment?

The questionnaires were sent to 543 women in Division 27. After making corrections for wrong addresses, men who were mistakenly included in the mailing, and others who were inappropriate for the survey, the sample included 510 women. There were 229 returned surveys that were usable in statistical analyses (45% of the sample) and an additional 15 partial returns or letters. Most participants had earned their doctorates (67%) or master's degrees (26%). Thus there is a clear sampling bias in that women who were effectively discouraged from completing their degrees were not among those surveyed. About 15% of the respondents were less than two years beyond their highest degree, about 25% were 2 to 5 years out, about 25% were 6 to 10 years, and another 25% were 11 to 21 years out. Eighteen (10.6%) obtained their degrees over 21 years ago. Most had completed clinical psychology graduate programs (74%).

Defining Sexual Harassment

The first goal of this survey was to better define what women experience as sexual harassment. Previous studies of psychology training by Glaser and Thorpe (1986), Pope, Levinson, and Shover (1979), and Robinson and Reid (1985) focused primarily on direct sexual contact, but such experiences are not necessarily synonymous with sexual harassment. Such a definition both includes sexual behavior that might not be experienced as harassment and excludes a broader range of less intimate behavior that, nonetheless, may be experienced as harassment (e.g., obscene comments, requests for dates). In order to assess a broad range of potentially sexually harassing behaviors, I developed a list of fifteen behaviors that could be construed as harassing. I drew from different policy definitions of harassment and also from Leidig's (1981) continuum of violent acts against women. This list includes behaviors ranging from jokes with sexual themes and sexist remarks to open invitations for sex and direct sexual contact. I not only asked about women's own experience of these behaviors in graduate training but also about: (1) their knowledge of others' experiences and (2) the extent to which they felt each behavior contributed to creating a training environment that was unsupportive of women. Respondents ratings of their own and others' experiences are summarized in the first two columns of Table 1.

The percentages of women who have experienced the harassing behaviors are quite high for almost every behavior assessed. The highest percentages are for behaviors such as jokes with sexual themes (75.0%), sexist comments that are demeaning to women (68.9%), sexist remarks directed at the individual's appearance (57.8%), and sexually suggestive kinds of remarks (56.8%). The lower percentages tend to be for those behaviors that involve actual sexual contact (12.2%), an open invitation (17.4%), or a more sexual kind of kiss (10.9%). These percentages, although lower than for other behaviors, nonetheless still indicate that sexual approaches and contact are experienced by at least one out of every 10 women respondents. The percentages of women aware of others' experience of these behaviors are, not surprisingly, even higher. These results indicate that when we get away from the notion that direct sexual contact or approaches are the only or primary type of sexual harassment, it becomes clear that sexually harassing types of behaviors are even more prevalent than we realized!

The EEOC definition of harassment includes any verbal or physical behavior which has the purpose or effect of "creating an intimidating, hostile or offensive work environment." These guidelines emphasize not just the occurrence of the behavior but also the impact the behavior has on the work environment. Thus to further enhance our understanding of the issue, it is important to look beyond the percentages indicating occurrence and to directly consider the extent the behaviors contribute to an unsupportive work/learning environment. The far right column of Table 1 summarizes the respondents' assessments of how much they think each behavior "contributed to creating a graduate training environment that was

Table 1
Potentially Sexually Harassing Behaviors
Experienced during Graduate Training

	% Experienced Behavior*	% Aware of Others Experiences**	Unsupport- iveness Ratings***
1. Jokes with sexual themes	75.0	84.0	3.44 (1.10)
2. Sexist comments demean- ing to women	68.9	74.7	4.32 (1.19)
3. Sexist remarks about your clothing, body, or sexual activities	57.8	74.7	3.88 (1.23)
4. Sexually suggestive com- ments	56.8	75.6	3.87 (1.23)
5. Staring at your body	49.6	69.8	3.77 (1.34)
6. Eye contact of a sus- tained/suggestive nature	39.2	56.0	3.58 (1.33)
7. Invitations for shared ac- tivities outside of work settings (just the two of you)	38.3	68.2	3.12 (1.21)
8. Quick kiss hello or good- bye	34.2	47.6	3.23 (1.36)
9. Subtle pressures for sex (e.g., joking, hinting)	32.4	66.8	4.04 (1.31)
10. Unnecessary touching, patting, or pinching	27.8	51.7	4.05 (1.38)
11. Invitation for dates	24.8	63.7	3.42 (1.29)
12. Open invitation for sex	17.4	50.6	3.97 (1.40)
13. "Accidental" physical con- tact with your sexual or genital body areas	14.6	35.4	4.04 (1.42)
14. Sexual contact (intercourse, breast, or genital stimulation)	12.2	45.1	3.97 (1.43)
15. Sustained and/or French kiss	10.9	30.4	3.92 (1.43)

* Percent indicating they experienced the behavior at least once during graduate training.

** Percent indicating they were aware of others experiencing the behavior at least once during graduate training.

*** Mean rating (and s.d.) of contribution to creating a "graduate education environ- ment that was unsupportive of women" (5-point scale from "never" to "always").

unsupportive of women." The behaviors with the highest mean un-supportiveness ratings include sexist comments that are demeaning to women, subtle pressure, and unnecessary or "accidental" touching. Direct sexual approaches and contact are also described as having a consistently negative impact on the learning environment and thus creating environments that are unsupportive of women's professional development. Although the differences in ratings are not great, a few behaviors are rated as somewhat less consistently negative in their impact. These ratings are some acknowledgment that there are situations where some types of potentially harassing behaviors, e.g., quick kiss hello/goodbye, invitation for shared activities, do not have sexual or threatening overtones. These results indicate that we need a multifaceted definition of harassment that takes into account the impact on the broader environment.

Radiating Impact

Part of assessing the impact of these behaviors on educational environments involves looking beyond the women who are direct victims and assessing the affect of sexual harassment on women who are simply aware of the behavior happening in their department. The mean ratings of "unsupportive impact" by those who directly experienced the behavior are almost identical to, and in some cases slightly lower than, ratings by those who did not. Thus it appears that direct experience of sexual harassment may not be the key factor in determining impact. In order to look at the correlations between experience of harassment and assessments of environmental impact, the original list of fifteen behaviors were factor analyzed and reduced to two summary variables for respondents' own experiences: subtle harassment and overt sexual behavior. The "subtle harassment" variable included behaviors such as jokes, suggestive comments, and subtle pressure. The "overt sexual behavior" variable included: direct invitations for dates or sex, sustained kisses, and actual sexual contact. A single factor emerged for ratings of others' experiences. Analyses reveal no correlations between ratings of environmental impact and direct experience of either subtle harassment or overt sexual approaches (Table 2). There is, however, a significant relationship between the extent of awareness of others' experiences and assessments of unsupportive environmental impacts. Environmental impact thus appears to be more consistently related to awareness of sexual harassment than to one's

Table 2
Correlations between Sexual Harassment
and Its Impact on the Environment

	Unsupportive Impact of Harassment Behaviors on Environment
Subtle Harassment	.11
Overt Harassment	.05
Harassment of Others	.24**

own direct experience. These results may speak to the diversity and complexity of reactions to being harassed, but they also underscore the fact that sexual harassment has a more consistently negative impact that radiates out beyond direct targets to many in the graduate school setting.

Sexual Harassment and the Environment

An ecological approach to the issue demands that we consider how sexual harassment relates to other environmental factors. In addition to clarifying definitions and examining prevalence statistics, we need to better understand what qualities of the educational environment contribute to or inhibit sexual harassment. To examine this question, six types of environmental variables were identified as potentially important in the occurrence of sexual harassment in educational settings. They are (1) departmental norms with respect to sexual relationships between educators and students; (2) formal acknowledgment of sexual harassment as an ethical issue, i.e., through coverage in courses or other components of the graduate program; (3) the availability of formal complaint mechanisms (i.e., policies and grievance procedures (not necessarily the use, but whether or not people were aware of and/or saw formal avenues as accessible); (4) the percent of women faculty; (5) the percent of women students in the program; and (6) the supportiveness of the program to women's professional development in general. Multiple regressions were used to examine the predictive ability of the six types of environmental variables to the occurrence of both subtle and overt harassment.

The main predictor of subtle harassment was the general reaction of department members to sexual contact between educators and students (Table 3). The percent of women students was also

Table 3
Determinants of Subtle Harassment

Variable	R^2	Regression Coeffiecient	Standard Error	F
Reaction of department	.049	1.80	.704	6.52*
Percent women students	.025	−0.07	.307	3.45+
Total	.074			5.05**

marginally predictive ($p < .10$). These results indicate that norms within a department that communicate disapproval of sexual relationships between faculty and students also may inhibit subtle harassment. Lower rates of subtle harassment also seem to be related to the program's orientation toward women. Percentage of female students and the extent to which an educational environment is seen as supportive of women's professional development are both positively correlated with occurrence of subtle harassment ($p < .001$) even though only marginally predictive in the multiple regression (Table 5).

The only significant predictor of overt sexual approaches appears to be the reaction of others in the program to faculty-student sexual contact (Table 4). Open disapproval is predictive of fewer incidents of overt sexual harassment. This again indicates that the general judgment of the environment about faculty-student relationships has a role in the incidence of these potentially harassing behaviors.

In sum, sexual harassment is a serious problem within graduate training programs in psychology. A broad range of potentially sexually harassing behaviors occur with alarming frequency. To fully understand the extent of the problem, we must consider both direct sexual contact and also a variety of more indirect and subtle forms of harassment. Using an inclusive definition helps in understanding

Table 4
Determinants of Overt Sexual Approaches

Variable	R^2	Regression Coeffiecient	Standard Error	F
Reaction of Department	.023	.510	.273	3.48+
Formal discussions about harassment situation	.017	−.478	.324	2.17
Total	.039			2.63+

Table 5

Correlations between Sexual Harassment and Environmental Variables

	1	2	3	4	5	6	7
1. Subtle Harassment	χ						
2. Overt Sexual Approaches	.50***	χ					
3. Percent Women Students	−.24***	−.09	χ				
4. Percent Women Faculty	−.10	−.05	.28***	χ			
5. Supportiveness of Women's Professional Development	−.25***	−.04	.31***	.22**	χ		
6. Reaction of Department	.20*	.15+	−.01	−.17*	−.06	χ	
7. Avenues for Formal Complaints	−.02	−.01	.27***	−.03	.10	−.03	χ
8. Formal Discussion about Harassment Situation	−.08	−.14*	.25***	.07	.09	.06	.30***

*** $p<.001$
** $p<.01$
* $p<.05$
+ $p<.10$

both the nature and the pervasiveness of the problem. We also need to recognize that the impact of sexual harassment is not limited to immediate targets. Most forms of harassment appear to have a radiating impact and thus can affect the educational experiences of all women in a program. This radiating impact needs to be considered in the development of policies and in the design of any preventive efforts. Departmental norms about faculty-student relationships as well as the presence of women within the program appear to be important environmental influences in the occurrence of the problem. Thus, we can all contribute to addressing the problem of sexual harassment by participating in defining a graduate context that promotes women's professional development and discourages abuses of faculty-student relationships.

Acknowledgment

(This paper is based on a presentation made at the 1987 APA meeting in New York. *Sexual harassment: A barrier to women's professional development in community psychology.*)

References

Bond, M. A., & Linney, J. A. (1986). *Women in community psychology: Status report and challenges for the field.* Paper presented at the meeting of the American Psychological Association, Washington, D.C.

Glaser, R., & Thorpe, J. (1986). Unethical intimacy: A survey of sexual contact and advances between psychology educators and female graduate students. *American Psychologist, 41* (1), 43–51.

Pope, K., Levenson, H., Shover, L. (1979). Sexual intimacy in psychological training. *American Psychologist,* 682–89.

Robinson, L., & Reid, P. (1985). Sexual intimacy in psychology revisited. *Professional Psychology: Research and Practice, 16* (4), 512–20.

O   APPENDIX **8**

Women's Explanations of their Harasser's Motivations

By Peggy Crull. Reprinted, with permission from the Community Psychologist.

Explorations of the causes of sexual harassment have taken place primarily within the sociological framework specifically within the structure of the workplace and the workforce. (Crull, 1987; Tangri, Burt; & Johnson, 1982). Many theorists working within that framework have proposed that male economic power engenders sexual harassment. Using a number of analytic approaches, they have found two common patterns of sexual harassment which represent two different ways in which male economic power leads to sexual harassment. In the first, the quid pro quo situation in which a boss with the authority to hire or fire propositions his female employee and denies her some job benefit when she fails to comply, the harassment appears to be the exercise of a right the man feels he has based on his work status. In the second situation, harassment comes in the form of sexually derogatory comments and behaviors that create an unpleasant or hostile atmosphere and tends to occur in formerly all-male workplaces. Here sexual harassment seems to be a tactic on the part of the men to regain a status at work that is waning (Crull, 1987).

My colleagues at Working Women's Institute and I began to wonder if these analyses were shared by the women who came to us for help in resolving a sexual harassment situation when one of the Institute's counselors noted that these women did not appear to attribute the actions of their harassers to any power that flowed from their jobs. Instead, according to the counselor, they emphasized aspects of the harasser's psychological make-up in explaining the

199

harassment. Specifically, they implied that the harasser's behavior was an outgrowth of some psychological inadequacy, peculiarity, or even pathology on his part, giving examples of the harasser's unappealing demeanor and style of operation to illustrate their point. Some of these examples were compelling enough to make us wonder ourselves if sexual harassment was not perhaps the product of a group of social misfits in the workplace rather than a symptom of unequal economic power between the sexes.

We decided to explore these two apparently conflicting hypotheses by interviewing some of the counselees to elicit their ideas of what caused the harassment they experienced.

Background Information

The Interview. An interview schedule which covered many aspects of the sexual harassment situation was constructed. Of the approximately 100 questions asked, five of them dealt with the woman's explanations of the origins of the sexual harassment. The specific hypothesis discussed here was addressed by the questions: "Did you ever ask, why did he start this in the first place?" and "Did you ever ask yourself, why did all of this happen to me?"

The Subjects. Twenty-eight of the more than 500 women that had contacted Working Women's Institutes for information, referrals, and counseling at that time were interviewed. Since it was not clear what factors would be the major determiners of their perceptions of the sources of the harassment, we decided to select women from a variety of racial and class backgrounds, in a variety of occupations, who had experienced a range of sexual harassment situations, rather than pick a sample that was representative of our client population on any one of these criteria.

The women's occupations fell into the following categories: Professional/Technical Workers (5), Managers/ Administrators (7), Sales Workers (2), Clerical Workers (11), Craft Workers (1), and Service Workers (2).

The women in the sample worked in business, government, and not-for-profit organizations including private schools and colleges. The organizations ranged in size from small to massive. One woman was self-employed. A large majority of the women in this sample were white-collar workers, but 3 were in blue-collar, male-dominated jobs. None were in male-dominated, professional/technical or managerial/administrative positions.

Twenty-two of the women were harassed by their bosses, men who, in many cases, had the sole authority to make decisions about the woman's job status. In fact, six of the men were the owners of their own businesses. In four cases the harasser was a co-worker, subordinate, or client. The woman who was self-employed was being harassed by a major customer. Finally, one woman was harassed both by her boss and by her co-workers.

Additional information about the harassment situation is useful here. In 25 of the cases the harasser was married. The average age of the harassers was approximately 48 years old where as the average age of the women was 34 years old.

The Nature and Outcomes of the Sexual Harassment.

A large majority (22) of these cases involved outright or subtle propositions to have sex. (In two instances the woman had begun a dating relationship with the harasser but attempted to end it. In another case the woman was coerced into having sexual intercourse with her harasser several times.) In five of the cases there was no direct proposition but simply embarrassing or derogatory sexual language and behavior. In both the cases of propositions and the cases of embarrassing and derogatory atmosphere, sexual touching sometimes accompanied the other actions. Finally, in one case the woman was experiencing difficulty on her job simply because she was friends with a woman who had ended an affair with her boss.

In 11 of the cases the women were fired, laid off, or demoted. In one case the woman was transferred. In ten of the cases the woman quit. In six of the cases there was no change in the woman's job status.

Data Analysis. For the present study we did a content analysis of the responses to the question about why the harasser started the situation and the answers to the question about why the woman thought the situation occurred. First we looked for how many of the women attributed the harassing behavior to the harasser's psychological make-up. Then we looked for evidence that the women attributed the harassment to sociological rather than individual psychological sources, in particular, the structure of the workplace or workforce. Finally, we sought out and attempted to categorize any additional themes which might emerge.

Four major categories of explanations of the origins of the harassment emerged. They were (1) explanations attributing the harassment to the harasser's own psychology, (2) explanations attributing the harassment to the harasser's power and authority derived through the work relationship, (3) explanations attributing the harassment to the attitudes arising out of the male gender role and, (4) miscellaneous explanations.

Women's Explanations of the Harassment

The women's explanations of the harassment were complex, usually attributing the situation to more than one factor. Because of this, there were 42 different responses given by the 28 subjects. These responses fell into the four categories in the following proportions:

Harasser's Psychology. Ten women alluded to the harasser's psychology, in much the same fashion as had been noted by the Working Women's Institute counselor, in explaining why he had harassed her. They mentioned aspects of the harasser's personality, usually personal problems or peculiarities, as the source of the behavior. Several women mentioned insecurity or other forms of emotional immaturity:

> "His own insecurities, He's a weirdo."
> "Insecurity."
> "He's emotionally ruled."
> "He's an irresponsible, immature human being."

Some noted more serious problems:

> "He had a problem with drinking.
> He was sick. Everyone would agree with that"
> "Maybe he just snapped."

Among these ten women who felt their sexual harassment was the result of a weakness of the harasser's psychology were several women for whom the sexual behavior in and of itself seemed to be a sign of his personal problems:

> "I met a creep."
> "He's a sick man. I feel sorry for him.
> He has nobody to help him."

Power Derived from the Work Relationship. Thirteen women mentioned some aspect of the harasser's or their own work situation as an explanation for the harassment. Of those 13, several of the responses clearly reflect the ideas in the literature that men harass as an outgrowth of the power they have at work. For example:

"He figured he was the boss and could get away with it."
"His attitude was, this is my center, you do what I say."
"He has everything, why not you?"

Two of the women who were in non-traditional jobs expressed the second theme in the literature, that their harassers felt their power threatened by the presence of a woman:

"He doesn't like taking orders from a women."
"I'm a woman in a non-traditional job."

Several other women who were not in non-traditional jobs also expressed the feeling that their harassers harassed them because they didn't know how to deal with competent women. For example:

"He doesn't understand what a professional black woman is like today."

The Male Gender Role. A third category emerged clearly from these answers, which, like the work category, was also sociological rather than strictly psychological. Eleven women proposed that the harassing behavior was an outgrowth of the male gender roles. About half of this group implied that such behavior is characteristic of all men or of certain types of men:

"Men are macho. They see women only as sex objects."
"He's an old-fashioned man. Any woman is fair game."

The other half seemed to indicate that the behavior came as a result of this particular man's attitude toward women as a group. For example:

"It's his way of getting out his hatred toward women."
"It's a power trip, a whole conquest thing. I'm the man. I'm stronger than you."

Miscellaneous Responses. Finally, there were eight responses which represented eight additional types of explanations. For example, one woman blamed the behavior of her harasser on the fact that another woman at work had gone to bed with him. Another woman felt her boss was moved by interest in her personal well-being and felt sorry for her because she was alone. Each of the 8 responses could represent a separate category of response, but since there was only one of each, we did not develop these categories.

Discussion

Contrary to the speculations of the Working Women's Institute staff that women being counseled for sexual harassment would attribute the behavior of their harassers primarily to their individual psychological peculiarities, the women in the present sample see a mixture of factors as the source of sexual harassment, with psychological peculiarities being the third most frequently mentioned one. The most common type of reason given by this group for their harassers' behavior was that they had or were fearful of losing power at work. Following this in popularity was the idea that male gender roles lead to harassing behavior. The idea that the harassment resulted from the harasser's psychological weaknesses or peculiarities was a close third, however, indicating that, indeed, there may be a number of males among our sample's harassers who were moved to act by some sense of social inadequacy.

This configuration of responses suggests an analysis of the origins of sexual harassment, or at least some incidents of sexual harassment, which combines the three explanations proffered by our sample. Perhaps the structure of the workplace provides an opportunity for men who feel psychologically and socially powerless to express the sexual aggressiveness of the male gender role that they would be afraid to express outside of that context. The power and authority they have through their jobs provides both an opportunity to act and protection from consequences they may not feel they have in the larger social world. A similar theory has been put forth by Dziech and Weiner in their analysis of sexual harassment on the college campus (Dziech & Weiner, 1984). They suggest that young female college students may serve as a convenient vehicle through which their professors can work out their never-resolved adolescent fantasies, their disappointments with their professional status, or their mid-life crises.

The analysis presented here is, of course, only suggestive. More extensive analysis of the interview on which the study is based will lead to a more thorough understanding of this particular group of women's perceptions of their harassers. In addition, of course, other methodologies for looking at the sociological and psychological factors which produce sexual harassment must be explored.

Acknowledgment

The research for this paper was conducted while the author was Research Director of Working Women's Institute, a national center for research, education, and training on sexual harassment and gender bias. The research was funded by Exxon. The work discussed here was the result of the efforts and analysis of the entire staff of the Institute. Special thanks go to Katie Taylor who first made the observations of our counseling clients which led to the present study, Suzanne Carothers who conducted the interviews, and Marilyn Cohen, Carmen Velasquez, Alyssa Haywood, and Joan McNamara who conducted the data analysis. Finally, we extend our appreciation to the women who participated in the interviews.

References

Crull, P. (1987). Searching for the causes of sexual harassment: An examination of two prototypes. In Bose, Feldberg, and Sokoloff (Eds.), *The hidden aspects of women's work*. New York: Praeger.

Dziech, B. W., & Weiner, L. (1984). *The lecherous professor: Sexual harassment on campus*. Boston: Beacon Press.

Gutek, B. (1985) *Sex and the workplace*. San Francisco: Jossey-Bass.

Tangri, S., Burt, M., & Johnson, L. (1982). Sexual harassment at work: Three explanatory models. *Journal of Social Issues, 38*, 33–54.

Sexual Harassment and the Law

By Midge Wilson. Reprinted with permission from the
Community Psychologist.

Academic administrators have recently been establishing policy statements on sexual harassment. Typically this task has included writing: a formal definition of sexual harassment, the college's or university's position with regard to engaging in such behavior, procedures for documenting these kinds of grievances, and the sanctions for founded charges. These policy statements are then disseminated throughout the campus by widespread education campaigns. In fact, these are the very recommendations recently issued by The American Council on Education. If you are a college student or a professor, then you very likely have observed your school recently issue some policy statement on sexual harassment. If you have not, then you almost certainly will soon.

Why, you might ask, are college administrators suddenly becoming so concerned about the problem of sexual harassment? After all, like football, it has been a tradition on the college campus for years. Many of us would like to believe that the voices of thousands of harassed college women have at least been heard. However, the more likely and parsimonious explanation is that institutions of higher learning are suffering intense litigation anxiety. In recent court cases, sexual harassment has been ruled both a violation of basic civil rights, and a barrier denying equal access to educational opportunities. Consequently, institutions are at risk for being sued for failure to provide faculty, administrators, staff, and students equal protection under the law. This article will review the history of these court rulings and speculate on their meaning for those of us on the college campus.

In the early 1970s, the federal courts began to deal with litigation on sexual harassment. The first sexual harassment case to actually reach the Supreme Court, after years of appeals, was *Meritor Savings Bank, FSB v. Vinson* in the summer of 1986. Mechelle Vinson, who was a former employee of the bank, charged Meritor Savings Bank with sexual discrimination under Title VII of the 1964 Civil Rights Act. Title VII specifically has to do with employment practices, and it states that it is an unlawful practice for an "employer" to discriminate against applicants or employees on the basis of race or sex (or religious preference, etc.). Over the four-year course of her employment with the bank, from 1974 until her resignation in 1978, Vinson felt that she had been a target of discrimination because of the constant sexual harassment she received from her supervisor. She testified that she ultimately acquiesced to his sexual advances out of fear that her continued refusal would result in loss of employment. In their defense, bank officials contended that they should not be held liable because the alleged sexual harassment by her supervisor had not been brought to their attention. They also produced evidence that Ms. Vinson had on occasion dressed in a provocative fashion and, in the end, they implied that her charges of sexual harassment were just another case of love gone sour. The lower court decision supported the bank's claim and ruled that Vinson was not the victim of sexual harassment because her relationship with her supervisor was voluntary. However, both the U.S. Court of Appeals and later the Supreme Court overturned the lower court's decision and ruled that Vinson's charges of grievance were warranted. The Court further upheld the principle that sexual harassment was indeed a violation of Title VII and that such a charge could be predicated on the basis of a sexually hostile environment that did not have to include the threat of actual loss of "economic" or "tangible" job benefits. In other words, a woman did not have to prove that a male supervisor had threatened her job security if she failed to have sex with him—only that his advances had been persistent and unwelcome.

Actually, the *Meritor Savings Bank, FSB v. Vinson* ruling was in keeping with the legal guidelines adopted in 1980 by the Equal Employment Opportunity Commission (EEOC). The EEOC defines sexual harassment broadly to include any unwelcome sexual conduct that is either (1) "made . . . a term or condition of an individual's employment" or (2) "has the purpose or effect of unreasonably interfering with an individual's work performance or creating an intimidating, hostile, or offensive working environment." Thus,

Meritor Savings Bank, FSB v. Vinson, being the test case, began to clarify some of the issues.

Sexual harassment by fellow employees, those equal to or even inferior to the harassed victim in job rank or status, is almost as pervasive as harassment by supervisory personnel. Were employees to be protected from co-worker harassment as well? Under the EEOC guidelines, an employer is liable for co-worker harassment when the claimant can demonstrate that the employer knew or should have known. The case of *Continental Can Co. v. State* is an example of what is meant by this EEOC guideline. In this case, a female employee of Continental Can informed her supervisor that certain, then unnamed, co-workers were constantly subjecting her to sexually derogatory remarks and verbal sexual advances. She was told "there was nothing that could be done and that she had to expect such behavior when working with men." She then filed suit and the Court ruled that the employer's failure to respond promptly to known occurrences of sexual harassment was discriminatory. She won the case and thus another legal issue surrounding sexual harassment was resolved. (Incidentally, it has not yet been determined to what extent educational institutions are legally responsible for students harassing fellow students. Like a lot of these issues, this likely will be resolved in some future court case.)

The case of *Katz v. Dole* also made it clear that an employer's response to incidents of sexual harassment must include "appropriate corrective action" that is designed to be "reasonably calculated to end the harassment." Employer action that was not so calculated was found to have occurred when Katz, a female air traffic controller, found herself the object of verbal sexual harassment by her fellow controllers. When she informed one of FAA's supervisory personnel of the problem, he not only did nothing effectual to stop it, he took part in the harassment by suggesting, among other things, that her complaint might be solved if she submitted to him. The Court noted that although the agency had articulated a policy against sexual harassment under a program involving seminars on the issue, its supervisory personnel knew that the policy was something of a joke. Thus, the Court upheld the plaintiff's claim that no significant effort was ever made to end her harassment.

So what is the situation regarding sexual harassment in academia? Many college and university administrators have been prompted to take a good, hard look at their own policies and procedures regarding sexual harassment. Their policies are partly influenced by Title VII because educational institutions are businesses and thus employees may file suit under this law. In addition, student-victims may seek relief under Title IX of the Educational amendments of 1972. Title IX, with which many of you may be familiar from the uproar it caused in mandating equal treatment (i.e., money spent) in men's and women's sports programs, actually applies to any educational program or activity that receives federal funds. Since nearly all colleges and universities rely on some form of federal assistance, it serves to protect most students (as well as the employees of the recipient institutions). Thus far, the only Title IX ruling directly addressing sexual harassment of students is the *Alexander v. Yale University* case filed in 1977. In this case, an undergraduate women charged she received a lower grade for refusing a professor's sexual overtures. Although this case was not successfully resolved from the students perspective, it did maintain that sexual harassment may constitute sexual discrimination under Title IX (cf. Dzeich & Weiner, 1984). The Office of Civil Rights (OCR) in the U.S. Department of Education, which administers Title IX, now requires institutions to maintain grievance procedures that provide "prompt and equitable" resolution of all complaints alleging sexual discrimination or harassment. In addition, recipient institutions must provide notice to employees and students of its grievance policy and procedures. If educational institutions do not have effective policies in place, a student may file a lawsuit. This was the case at the University of Pittsburgh where a former graduate student charged that she could not get help with a harassment complaint because the university lacked proper procedures. At risk to the institutions, if a sexual harassment problem is found and not resolved, is the federal financial assistance which it receives. Thus, students, like employees, have a legal right to an environment free of sexual harassment.

Since most of us will never go to the trouble of contacting a lawyer and filing a lawsuit for our grievances of sexual harassment, how do these federal acts and court cases affect the daily life of the average student trying to get through school without feeling the pressure of harassment? Will any of all this make a difference to her (or him)? Both yes and no. According to Anne Truax, director of the Women's Center at the University of Minnesota, "harassment policies soon will be as common as tenure codes and any institution that doesn't have a policy is asking for trouble." Thus, because college and university officials have been forced to write these policies and to deliberate on these issues, students' complaints of sexual harassment will be taken much more seriously than in the past. Professors also will be made more aware of the consequences of their harassing actions and, as a result, many will think twice before engaging in some behavior that puts them at risk for losing their tenure. On the negative side, however, harassment will not go away overnight just because the school passed some policy on it. But the issue has come out of the closet, and there are some things that students can and should learn to do to directly and effectively stop harassing behavior when it occurs. (In my examples, I will use the prototype of a male instructor harassing a female student, although it is recognized that other patterns of harassment exist.)

If a faculty member inappropriately comments on a student's dress or appearance, she should not smile or look away. She should immediately respond with something like, "I thought I was here today to discuss my paper." She should always try to deal with situations as they happen, before they escalate. If an instructor makes an objectionable comment in class about women, perhaps a response like the following would work: "I'm a woman and I don't feel or act that way. Do you have research supporting that point of view?" If an instructor tries to inappropriately touch her, she could confront him with something like this, "I don't touch you, please don't touch me." Then if he laughs and says, "Well, honey, you can touch me anytime." she should reply, "The point is simply that I prefer not being touched by you, and I hope that you can respect that." In other words, she should worry less about his ego and worry more about her own preferences and self-worth. She also should keep an accurate record with the date, time and names of witnesses who observed repeated incidences of sexual harassment. And then if all these tactics fail, she should inform him that she has found his behavior unwelcome and persistent and, if it doesn't immediately stop, then she will have no choice but to file a complaint of sexual harassment. And should it be necessary, she should follow through on her ultimatum. After all, laws and sexual harassment policies won't help students unless they demonstrate a determination to use them.

This is not an easy thing to do as few of us want to carry around the guilt of knowing someone was reprimanded or lost their job over a complaint that we made, even if they were the ones who behaved improperly and perhaps broke the law. But, if enough people across the country can find the courage to directly confront those who harass us, then surely sexual harassment will become a thing of the past.

References

Dziech, B. W., & Weiner, L. (1984) *The lecherous professor: Sexual harassment on campus*. Boston: Beacon Press.

Index

213